WROUGHT IRON

739.4
74053

Hover, O.
Wrought iron.

OTTO HÖVER

Wrought Iron

ENCYCLOPEDIA OF IRONWORK

UNIVERSE BOOKS

Translated from the German by Ann C. Weaver
Original title: DAS EISENWERK

Third American edition published in the United States of America in 1969 by
UNIVERSE BOOKS, Inc., 381 Park Avenue South, New York 10016
The first edition of this book was published in 1927 by
E. Weyhe, New York under the title: „Encyclopedia of Ironwork"

———

Library of Congress Catalog Card No. 62-12006
© Verlag E. Wasmuth, Tübingen 1969
Printed in Germany

CONTENTS

LIST OF PLATES

VI

VIII

X

STYLE IN DECORATIVE WROUGHT-IRON WORK

Even if the most important achievements of smiths and locksmiths are rarely founded on original discoveries, decorative wrought iron is for the most part the finest practical embodiment of a linear idea. All the many possibilities for the designs of artistically wrought iron lead back to a basic linear element: the iron bar. More than one bar will produce mountings and grillework. Grillework is the ultimate object of all the technical and artistic work done by the masters of the guild of smiths. The iron mounting can be looked on as a safety grille riveted on to a solid background.

It almost seems as if important stylistic characteristics might already be inherent in the three main forms of the bar: the flat, the round and the square bar. Thus during the beginning and middle of the Gothic period the flat wrought-iron bar, in parts narrow and in parts wide, is favoured; but the round bar dominates the late Gothic period and, in the north, goes on into that period which we normally call the Renaissance. In the south, in Italy, the Renaissance brings with it the use of square bars. Likewise the Baroque period, under the leadership of the French craftsmen, turns to the square iron. These are the undisputed peaks of decorative wrought-iron work.

The ironwork of each period has a direct share in the general formation of the style prevalent at that time. It was so successful as the representation of natural and familiar forms that the late Gothic style was still being produced when other and more modern views had already long become standard in the other branches of the fine and applied arts. The late Gothic idea of line exists side by side with the Renaissance and Baroque forms for a long time, particularly in German work.

Attempts have been made to divide the complete development of decorative wrought iron since the Gothic period into two great stages: decorative and structural (cf. Adolf Brüning, *Die Schmiedekunst bis zum Ausgang des 18. Jahrhunderts.* 2nd edition, Alfred Rohde, Leipzig, 1922.) That is without a doubt correct. However, this division is a characteristic of any applied art. It touches the roots of artistic creation. The two principles are as old as the 'ornamental' craftsmanship of mankind in general. The decorative principle is like a method of filling in; the structural is like a dividing or framing method. The former is always possessed of a more dynamic character, and flamboyance decides the issue. In the latter, serenity reigns supreme, and eveything seems to be subdued and static and utterly stable. Thus the late Gothic in the north and the Italian Renaissance in the south – 'the art of beautiful and serene existence' (Wölfflin) – are diametrically opposed. Baroque and Rococo show the synthesis of the static and dynamic. The apportionment of the whole surface, the grille for instance, remains static and architectonic. But the surrounding parts, especially the cresting, develop into a ornamental design of exceptionally flamboyant motifs (strapwork and rocaille).

The varied artistic temperament of different nations is revealed in their treatment of the framework. The German idea of form triumphs in the late Baroque and Rococo, as it did in the late Gothic period, with a maximum of dynamic winged decoration, as opposed to the static and structural forms of Italian and French origin. The rigidity of the latticed inner part is surrounded by an almost formless profusion of framework. The frame was formerly something solid and straight which bonded the curving wealth of the inner design together rigidly and rectangularly, but now the relationship between frame and filling seems to be reversed: the filling has become serene and tectonic, and the framework vivaciously flamboyant. High above the arched cornice it is loosed and frees itself. Then it shoots up into the wide-open space, like flames from the glowing fire of the sun.

Then the final step is taken: the grille is made to appear three-dimensional. It takes on a spatial, a space-producing and space-preserving, function. While the basic linear character is still maintained, the third immaterial dimension is captured, over and above mere plasticity. This stage is reached in the latticework of those craftsmen of creative architecture, who made known, at a later date, all the secrets of three-dimensional design in both sacred and secular buildings of France and Germany.

The same principle can be applied to decorative wrought iron, as to all other ornaments in stucco, wood and other materials; the framework, as such, is still an essential part of artistic and imaginative design, but at the same time it not only surrounds a flat surface, but also has three-dimensional power. That is to say: the flamboyant ornamentation represents a framework of space. Only the dynamic, the eternally flamboyant, could have the last word here, in the same way that the architectonic space has also itself been something inwardly flamboyant and dynamic in the late Baroque and Rococo.

*

The art of the smith has always created works from 'graphic' examples – in the widest sense. Ornamentation in iron remained secondary to the inventiveness of artists and illuminators. At the beginning and middle of the Gothic period these illuminators were without a doubt superior in the graphic arts. What we admire in the mountings on the west portal of Notre Dame in Paris is an offshoot of the most highly developed illumination of books (marginal drawings and initials) from the time of St. Louis. A system of large spirals branching out into smaller spirals, ramifications and leaf and rosette-like terminations covers the whole surface and gives it a serene and almost classical appearance. The panel and the apportionment of the whole surface have become almost identical.

One is tempted to call the convoluted course of the tendrils and spiral motifs, 'romantic.' There is some truth in this. But the peak of the Gothic style in France was impregnated with the 'classical' spirit. The masters of cathedral sculpture (Rheims) usually kept very close to examples from antiquity. The treatment of the drapery, the modelling of the noble heads, even the whole stance of the figure are witnesses to this. The sketchbook of the French architect Villard d'Honnecourt of the mid-13th century has preserved some drawings which suggest an archeological study of the remains of antique statues.

We must imagine the models and books of contemporary smiths to be like the sketchbook of this much travelled and knowledgeable architect. But the main original model is to be found in illuminations.

Following the illumination of books at the height of the Middle Ages comes calligraphy. From the colorful abundance of illuminating emerges a style of pure quill drawing, which indulges in beautifully arching curves and twists. The smith now transposes the calligraphy of these pen-drawn examples into a system of straight and bent round bars. The 'skilled writer' takes the floor and determines the total character of the grille and its variations.

In the period of the Renaissance, calligraphy reaches a zenith in the imaginative marginal illustrations which Albrecht Dürer created for the prayer book of Kaiser Maximilian. The spirit of the late Gothic period in Germany held its own in its curling graphic work against the ideas of the Renaissance. These, based on foreign influences, strive after monumental and tectonic simplicity, imitating the great visual form of painting and sculpture: figures from the grave of Sebaldus by Peter Vischer, Dürer's pictures of the Madonna and apostles, Hans Holbein the Younger's portraits, and so on.

Not all decorative wrought-iron work of that time is in fact 'Renaissance.' The calligraphic style of iron ornamentation is secretly interspersed with and ruled by the vitality and flamboyance of the late Gothic idea of line. As long as the round bar is dominant, the late Gothic style is still dominant in the guild-bound craft of the smiths and locksmiths. The grille enclosing the grave of Maximilian in the *Hofkirche*, Innsbruck (c. 1570) is a product of that same spirit which produced the marginal illustrations of Dürer and his fellow artists for the prayer book of this cultivated German monarch.

The craft of wrought-iron work in Germany adheres to the calligraphic fashion until far into the 17th century. As in the case of many sacred buildings (Jesuit churches) of that period, one might speak of a 'posthumous' Gothic style. This is a sign of how firmly late Gothic was rooted in the German blood – German artistic talent really came into its own for the first time in the late styles. But on the other hand it is evidence of how much the bent round bar technically and materially accorded with the intentions of the smiths.

In Germany, the late Gothic and Baroque styles are

often contemporaneous. The history of the German formal imagination is in a special sense a history of the Baroque imagination. In Germany the Baroque style seems to be a continuation of the late Gothic using other media.

What is generally considered to be the arabesque of the so-called German 'Renaissance' actually reveals this overlapping of a late Gothic trend which is drawing to a close and a Baroque method which is coming to birth.

The German artistic and formal temperament always has to transform what is static and serene into something dynamic. At the height of the Middle Ages we find the 'classicism,' the comparative serenity of the French at the time as the Renaissance of the Italians. In both cases the Germans take up the reforms most suited to them. They succeed in producing their own characteristic artistic expression in all forms of ornamentation in the arts and crafts, just as they solved the greater and more comprehensive problems in architecture and the graphic arts.

During the course of the 17th century and the whole of the 18th century France is once again the model for Germany and indeed for the whole of Europe. Patterns for decorative wrought-iron work now find wide circulation through the works of the ornamental engravers. A great deal, and often the most important part, has been lost. Difficult and disturbed times in national and foreign politics caused wrought-iron works of art to be transformed into weapons. However, many engravings have been preserved which illustrate the change of form of that time, especially at the turn of the 17th to the 18th century. Here it is not actually the original designs of the smiths and locksmiths themselves which are in the lead, but the inventions of the architects and the 'professional designer' (cf. Brüning). The smiths certainly do produce their own models at this time, especially in France, but what they offer has the artistic achievements of the independent architectural and ornamental designers or graphic artists as a prior condition. The artistic craft of the smith is dependent on the patterns provided by the graphic arts. France is the undisputed leader here. Excellent

individual workmanship is already to be found by the mid-17th century. Some examples, like the remarkable book of Mathurin Jousse *La fidèle ouverture de l'art de Serrurier* for instance, appeared in the first half of the century (1627 at La Flèche). The works which came out about 1700 form the actual beginnings. Here, as in many other fields of the arts and crafts the engravings of the Frenchmen Daniel Marot and Jean Bérain acquire an epoch-making significance. The French call it *style régence*.

The German modification of French models of this time is aptly described as strap-work or ribbon-work. In this strap-work we can see the peculiar linear imagination of the German masters, just as it had been in the late Gothic and early Baroque scroll and grotesque work before the outbreak of the Thirty Years' War. The French always attached great importance to the serene superficial apportionment and tectonic stability of the appearance; the Germans, however, seek afresh the flamboyant panelling. At least the flamboyance with its most delightful details overruns the basic structural form of the inner section and framework. Just as in the Gothic period the round bar with its far-reaching effects was predominant, now we have the iron strap, the flat bar, which seems to contradict all that is best in the technique of wrought iron.

But the basic linear character remains just the same in these products, though the widest possibilities of linear profusion are attained. A quotation from Heinrich Wölflin is applicable to these products, that one can also 'think picturesquely in lines.' The great art critic was of course referring to the late Gothic medley of lines. But the new dynamic force of the flamboyant line in the strap-work is somehow spiritually and formally related to the late Gothic character.

Further development still follows the path indicated by the ornamental engravers. We shall come back to some peculiarities of flamboyant ornamentation when we reach the examples in the illustrations. For the present, we must simply mention the essential features on which the general development of the style of wrought iron depends.

THE GOTHIC PERIOD

During the 13th century the best decorative wrought-iron work was to be found in France. The smiths knew that they had to create something in iron whose ornamental value would match the architectural achievements of the Gothic cathedral. But as always in creative French art, where it has attained something alone – regardless of whether it is the height of the Middle Ages or in the *grand style* of Louis XIV – a distinctly rationalistic trait appears both in architecture and the applied arts. The vertical system of cathedrals, peculiar to France, reveals itself on closer examination as metaphysical. Everything is thought out and established by calculation. The way to God is directed along equal, mathematically arranged paths. The classical law of ancient tectonics has been thrown over by the northern people but the style of the French, especially in the well-ordered appearance and lucidity of all plastic arrangements in the interior of the cathedral, can be compared with the clarity of the Doric temple. One might even say that a basic 'classical' mood is inherent in the north of France, in the sphere of origin and domination peculiar to the Gothic cathedral. The Gothic design in building is not the result of an over-exuberant imagination. It is rather bound up with an *esprit technique* and rooted in *raison* in a constructional judgment. The logical conclusion of this is the enormous upright bars of iron of the 984 foot tower which the engineer Gustave Eiffel created centuries later on the Champ de Mars for the Paris exhibition of 1889.

Among all the unprecedented profusion of ornamental curves and spiral ramifications, the mountings on the portal of Notre Dame in Paris remain clear and distinct down to the last leaf-like terminations. The straps which are important to the construction and which, like compound stone pillars, are made up of bundles of flat bars, show their individual parts clearly everywhere. The volutes branch out upwards and downwards from these and form panels. Despite their curving flamboyance they are serene and controlled, not unlike the ornamental strap-work in ancient craftsmanship with spiral, undulating and meandering patterns. One can hardly detect anything of the so-called 'unending melody' of the Gothic line in this great design unprecedented in its wealth of imagination. However, the craftsmanship on the portal of Notre Dame is surpassed by a magnificent piece of wrought-iron work from Ourscamp abbey (cf. illustration).

There is certainly an unending melody characteristic of the Gothic. Yet its realization and a correspondingly dynamic character are reserved for the creative imagination of the Germans later in the Middle Ages. Not until then are these mysterious original forces of northern talent at work again, forces which had already operated before in the interlacing strap-work of animal ornamentation and in Irish manuscript illuminations.

In the Gothic period the French achieved absolute control over that native and original northern mode of fashioning which could so easily have been lost in formlessness, compared with the classical workmanship. Perhaps even then the 'Latin' spirit of this people, who were afterwards to join so whole-heartedly the Romanesque cultural alliance of the European peoples, was already asserting itself.

The genre of the decorative wrought-iron ornamental details of the French craftsmen, as shown in the illustrations, is completely Romanesque. The nature of French workmanship demands that flamboyant panelling be transformed into a clear and lucid articulation of the surface, by retaining the oldest individual motifs like the metal spirals which issue from the compound flat bars and terminate in leaf and rosette-like motifs. This produces the tendrils, and the comparison to the ancient motifs is thereby completed. The flat iron with its curving offshoots is forged anew for a short distance as a round bar. It then finishes in the wide and flat forms of leaves and rosettes. All material means of working are exploited, yet always in such a way that certain stylistic bounds of technical restraint are nowhere exceeded. The law of Gottfried Semper, that form is the result of material, skill and purpose, has found its noblest embodiment, though still lifted above the purely materialistic and mechanical idea on which the theorist of style in the mid-19th century based his formulation. In the healthy objectivity of a craftsman's trade the boundaries were known by a definite instinct. The vitality of an unbroken creativeness was still superior to the secondhand theories of imitators.

Even where the spiral motif of age-old metal workmanship is well preserved and suitably worked out, that is to say where the transformation into tendrils and the suffusion with organic and vegetable details (leaf, bunch of grapes, rosette) is not given, or a similarity with ancient forms seems to have been avoided, the French were successful at the turn of the 13th century, and also during the whole course of this century right into the 14th century, in transforming abstract curves of metallic material into serene and undynamic panelling. Specimens of this treatment of the surface are to be found in Rouen (window grilles) or on a fire-guard from the north of France and on the wrought-iron door of the cathedral at Le Puy en Velay (even from the end of the 12th century) (see Constantin Uhde, *Die Konstruktionen und die Kunstformen der Architektur*. Berlin, Wasmuth, 1911. Vol. IV, 2, pp. 83 ff.)

Side by side with the abstract spiral motifs which have no similarity with the motifs of vegetable and organic nature and which develop from widely spaced compound bars (i. e. whole groups of flat bars, unfurling in curves), we have other variations which form genuine S-scrolls and lead back to the basic form of a question-mark. Surrounded by a frame of solid and straight square bars and joined to the frame with square iron collars, these 'S' and 'question-mark' motifs produce a charming and rich pattern. The latticework is very closely meshed. The aim of security and seclusion has been completely attained. The incessant repetition of such monotonous motifs does, however, show an abatement of creative imagination, even if the greatest recognition is still due to the material handling. A grille so closely meshed is reinforced on the top by towering square rods with spikes. It resembles an armed force drawn up in rank and file – *las Lanzas!*

*

In comparison with the French ironwork at the peak of the Gothic period (13th century) the workmanship of German smiths of the same time and the epoch immediately following looks much more primitive. It is rougher work, yet full of originality and materialistic realism. In some respects the same contrasts are shown as between the elegant sculpture of the French cathedrals and the melancholic figures of German cathedrals, e. g. the statues of princes and knights in the west choir of Naumburg cathedral. Classical influence is absent. The Germans show a rustic humanity in contrast to the polished and cultivated urbanity of the French.

The same contrast is apparent in Hellenic antiquity between the heavy yet powerful Doric and the fine-limbed Ionic.

The French style is a perfected style. The German is undeveloped. The uncommonly rich development to follow is powerfully introduced with some striking works. When France had already put into practice the final achievements of the distinctive Gothic period, the first works of the new mediaeval style were just appearing in Germany. The German craftsmen from then on formed a definite style in architecture proper, and in the by-products of all branches of the arts and crafts including wrought-iron work.

While France has already attained to manifold connected and continuous scroll and tendril motifs whose curves develop from a stem, German mounting work has the flat bar as its basic element and is still made up of individual motifs which are riveted to the bottom in pure co-ordination. There are rectangular or diagonally crossing flat irons which terminate ornamentally, yet which are still abstractly restrained and hardly recognizable as any kind of vegetable pattern. For this various motifs are collected together which show C-motifs surrounding the crossed sections of the mounting on both sides. An example of this is to be found on the transept door of the convent church of Maulbronn (early 14th century) and – somewhat more primitive – on the main door of the same church dating from the early 13th century. On the latter example the rivet heads are also used as 'scatter ornamentation.' The total impression is fixed by the composition of C-scroll motifs alternating with simple or cross-shaped horizontal bars, something like the following pattern (–) (+).

Diagonally crossing flat irons are then used on city gates (Ronneburg near Büdingen). The gate is

1. Door in Durham cathedral, beginning of 13th century. 2. Door of the abbey church of Radford, Nottinghamshire, 13th century. 3. Door of Notre Dame, Orcival near Clermont, 12th century. 4. Hinge of a door from the abbey church of St. Albans, 1160–90 (Victoria and Albert Museum). 5. Hinge of a door in Merton College, Oxford, end of 13th century. 6. Door of the church in Hormead near Buntingford. 7. Door mounting from a house in Saffron Walden, Essex. 8. Lion's head on the north door of Le Puy cathedral, 11th century.

divided up in a diamond shaped pattern. Rosettes are used to fill the rhombic spaces between the ironwork. The rivet heads have ornamental qualities on the flat iron as well.

The mountings on the west door of the *Elisabeth-kirche* in Marburg and on the sacristy door of the parish church in Weilderstadt (Württemberg) are worthy of mention. In Marburg the strap-work is decorative and narrow. C-scrolls and cross motifs are charmingly varied and manifold. The terminations resolve into tendrils, with suggestions of leaf and rosette motifs. On the door at Weilderstadt the vertical iron bars branching up and down in triplicate determine this impression. The ends run into a triad of small ramifications which issue from small knotty extensions. The whole thing is like the longitudinal section of a calyx. A stem grows up straight in the center like a flower pistil. Two small branchlets which bend outwards are similar to rolled sepals or petals. But the total effect remains essentially abstract.

Some other portals of German churches are supplied with and made safe by brilliantly executed mountings on the principle of straight angular ramifications and forkings. Next to this come the spirals and volutes of French definition. Yet no compound and fluted flat irons are related here as in Notre Dame in Paris. It is a matter of an essentially limited formation, as for example on the left lancet of the north-east portal of Erfurt cathedral or on a cupboard door in the Town Hall at Erfurt. Of course the mountings with straight and angular ramifications seem more original. Pieces are added to the tendril-like bends of primary and secondary branches; leaf-like terminations are also to be found, similar to the foliage of an oak (for example, on the sacristy door at Marbach in Hessen) and rosette motifs, yet the character of the mountings as a whole has retained something of its abstractness and primitiveness (cf. door of Magdeburg cathedral, 14th century; Erfurt cathedral, etc.) The panelling seems rigid and unmovable, corresponding to the material, but not yet betraying anything of the dynamic force of decorative German wrought-iron work of the late Gothic period. Rustic simplicity decides the issue. The straps are riveted; the rivets have an ornamental role to play in the ironwork. Plaiting different flat irons and placing them on top of one another has for the most part been avoided.

German ironwork of this epoch seems to be completely *sui generis*. In contrast to the way the French iron is handled at the peak of the Gothic period as independent of other ornamental models, it is modelled on contemporary book illustrations, which, as has been shown, are conclusively relevant to the tendrils and scroll-work of French craftsmanship. (cf. a grille in the abbey church of St Yves at Braisne). When the zenith of wrought-iron formation had been achieved, France had already attained a final form of high Gothic style, while Germany was still in the process of forming a style.

Further development takes place more in grillwork, as opposed to pure mounting work. Here new points of view regarding design become authoritative. The grille is interspersed with motifs which are borrowed from architecture. It contains, in short, 'tracery,' like the divisions in the huge and rose windows of the cathedrals. The round bar is preferred to the flat iron. At the same time the square bar is an important basic element in military protection. In place of the spirals and the S- and C-scrolls, quatrefoil ornamentation appears on the round and square bars. Stone-tracery in architecture has become the example for the smiths.

Besides the division of the grille-work into several circles, filled in with quatrefoil motifs, we also find accurate imitations of sculptural window divisions. The grille is an imitation of the window with narrow upright sections which terminate in round or pointed arches and which are carried through to the upper part of the tracery. The whole thing is surrounded by richly profiled rigid frames. On the inside of these the round bar is dominant. This principle of tracery is carried out in all countries. An especially characteristic example from Florence (14th century) is shown in our illustrations.

In the course of development the fashioning of the inner sections of grilles and mountings follows the gradual changes in tracery, just as they originated from the imagination of the stonemasons. The flamboyant motif which was so extraordinarily loved in the later part of the Gothic period is also used as a centrepiece for grilles and mountings, mostly surrounded by a circle. Panelling now changes into a 'vibrant style' and becomes what is known as radiant *(rayonnant)* and flaming *(flamboyant)*, after the French. Those great rose windows which represent this type of pure culture are to be found in the

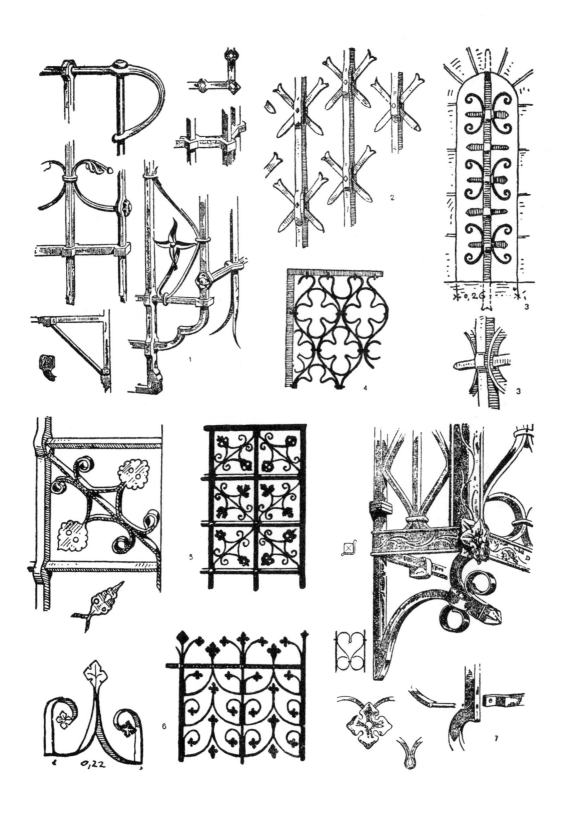

Mediaeval grille links.

XIX

French cathedrals of the later period (14th and beginning of the 15th century). Ironwork is duly influenced. Often the workmanship in this particular style seems like filigree or fret-saw work. In many cases the ornamentation will have been sawn or filed out of the iron. The detail often seems quite rough and harsh, but the total impression is sparkling, restless, almost punctulate. The bar-work itself is in the background, and so this type of ironwork had no significant future possibilities. Yet the pure grille-work made up of round and square iron bars remains the main element from whose original material potentialities new creations arise.

Some examples, in which the latticed inner section is not right-angled but diagonally crossed, are especially interesting materially. Strong square bars are threaded through one another in such a way that on the individual bars it is not the flat side but rather the pointed edge which faces outwards. Thus a pointed profile of the simplest design, thoroughly Gothic in intention, comes into being. Even the rhombic areas between the bars seem completely Gothic. Everything relies on the effect of the pure lattice-work. Ornamental additions are completely left out of the inner section. The shape of the edged iron alone remains essential. Only the wide frames, from which the grilles spring, are richly decorated, (grille in a monstrance in the Hamburg *Museum für Kunst und Gewerbe*). In other cases the places where the grille joins the frame, the rivetings are emphasized decoratively with small rosette motifs and therefore concealed.

The diagonal crossing of the bars, the so-called cross-patterning, with the individual bars threaded closely in and out of one another, becomes characteristic for the works made up of round iron bars. This type of simplest lattice-work endures as long as the round bar remains the most important element in the grille, in fact, right into the 16th century. The round bar is the peculiar medium of late Gothic work.

The new curving course of the iron bars is essential and with it a new dynamic style of panelling which abandons the previous ornamental excitement. Notable examples of the simplest cross-patterning of the period from the 14th to the 16th century are the grilles for the shrine of Elizabeth in Marburg as well as parts of a grille from Hall in the Tyrol. Both these grilles are especially distinguished by the rich style of the upper cresting; in Marburg, finial plant and leaf motifs of 'carved and painted iron' with figurative ornamentations; in Hall, keel-arch motifs of diagonally crossing square bars in every conceivable variation, and with finial vertical terminations, filled with small ornamentations using heraldic motifs and knightly emblems, helmet decorations and other such things. The simple grille is therefore protected by the pointed ornamentation in the most effective way at the top from intruders who might climb over it. An intruder would be caught without hope of escape in the Gothic scroll work and sustain heavy injuries. The grille surface, without decorative embellishments, is calm; but the ornamental imagination in the upper frames is completely dynamic – a method often used in the Baroque period. Calm, static inner form together with flamboyant framework and cresting produce, by their conscious antagonism, effects which do justice in a direct way to all the potentialities of wrought-iron work.

Late Gothic, especially the German version of it and its effects, was not solely concerned with complicating the frames and crestings of the grilles in a dynamic way. The real problem was to impregnate even the inner section which is filled with lattice-work with the greatest measure of curved design. Architectonic motifs – the forms borrowed from architecture proper – become less and less important. The calligraphic scroll and spiral work of the book illuminators and scribes again becomes the standard. The Gothic style is really properly perfected for the first time. Northern linear imagination finds a peculiar fulfilment in the bent and curving iron, wrought by the hand of the smith and locksmith.

Grille from Florence, 15th century.

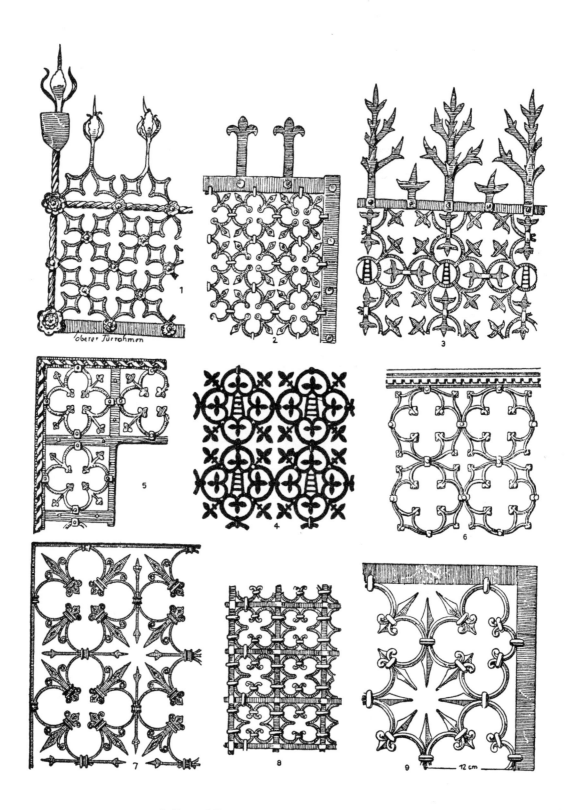

Italian and French grilles, 13th and 14th centuries.
1. Church at Langeac, upper section of chapel grille, c. 1400. 2. San Marco, Venice (gilt), 13th century. 3. and 4. Verona, tombs of the Scaligers, 1300–1380 (overall height about 8 ft. 6 ins). 5. and 6. Town Hall in Siena, 14th century. 7. French tabernacle grille (gilt), 14th century. 8. French, 13th century(?) in the Musée des arts décoratifs, Paris. 9. From Brescia, 14th century.

XXII

THE RENAISSANCE

The line in iron grille ornamentation, outside Italy, acquires its own nuances in contrast to the more plastic and physical conception of ironwork among the Italians.

After-effects of the Gothic conception do certainly remain in evidence in Italy until far into the 15th century (Quattrocento). But architecture and architectonics gradually take the lead again. The architectonic conception, the idea of construction of the Italians and Southerners, had at that time turned completely to the plastic ideal, especially in the outer building. The shell of the building was conceived as a space-producing structure. The building of the Italians under the leadership of Brunelleschi, Leon Battista Alberti, Bramante and all the others, again came close to the buildings of antiquity.

The cubic shape of a Palazzo or of a cupola above a symmetrical building forms a harmonious plastic whole. From the planes of walls and their own tectonic resources they conjured forth the symmetry seen in the Doric pillars on the Greek temples which has achieved universal validity. The stones themselves, particularly in functional palace buildings of Tuscany, were perfectly handled and formed for the plastic potentialities of the monumental stone buildings. The Pitti and Strozzi palaces will always be proof of this.

It is no surprise that this plastic conception was transferred to the handling of *all* raw materials. The grilles, fitted to the windows for defense purposes, especially on the ground floor, and made from interwoven square bars crossing at right angles, seem absolutely solid. Something which was originally linear has now reached the point of greatest solidity. This is a maximum of plasticity in contrast to the minimum of plasticity in the linearity of the late Gothic period. Indeed, the Baroque, and in its wake the Rococo period, was to reach yet a further stage in the development of plastic solidity in ironwork. This stage of maximum plasticity is historically presupposed and conditioned by the Italianate stage of the Renaissance. It develops originally from it, both in

monumental tectonics and architectonic décor as well as in all ornamental raw materials and in decorative wrought iron.

Beside the latticing of the windows, it is above all the decorative wrought-iron flag holders (ring-shaped holders) and lanterns which clarify plastic intention in Italian ironwork. The famous lanterns (for example from the *Palazzo Guadagni* in Florence) seem like small tabernacles; the smallest possible constructions centered on a polygon base (eight sided), imitating the outward appearance of the great symmetrical buildings.

The symmetrical building was the absolute ideal of the Italian Renaissance. The cresting of the great cupolas was simply marked by the suggestion of a lantern. The wrought-iron lanterns on the palace façades are not differently planned and developed from these lanterns built high above the round or polygonal cupolas. Piers, pilasters and pillars – in miniature to be sure – determine the basic tectonic structure even of the decorative iron lanterns. The openings on the eight sides are treated as arcades. Minute decorative baluster pillars form a balustrade; a richly decorated entablature produces the horizontal termination in the remaining part with slight mouldings at the corners. Above this the mighty spikes form a cresting: the middle one stiff and straight, those on the sides bent outwards.

It almost seems as if in such work, especially flag holders, door-knockers, and similar forms of decoration, the material character of the wrought iron has been obliterated. Loans have been made in the casting technique to make sure of the desired plastic effect. The masterly achievements in bronze casting and embossed work, in the way that the sculptors of the Quattrocento from Lorenzo Ghiberti and Donatello to Verrocchio had perfected them, offered the necessary and natural models for the treatment of iron. Verrocchio himself produced the highest achievement in the bronze grille for the old sacristy of San Lorenzo in Florence. The lattice-work imitates, in bronze, interwined ropes. Even the acanthus ornamentation on the sarcophagus for Piero and Giovanni de' Medici which stands under the grille, anticipates in bronze much that is later to be imitated in iron by the smiths.

The plastic conception of the architects and builders continually determines the shape of ironwork. Plastic completeness is 'Renaissance' in the full and real sense of the word. The curved and spiral work of the smith outside Italy during the 15th and 16th centuries is diametrically opposed to the Renaissance conception. There is in it a linear idea which is still late Gothic. It is not architects and builders who determine the ornamental treatment of the grille-work and the dynamic tendency of the curved features; the calligraphic artists of whom the greatest exponents were Martin Schongauer, and Albrecht Dürer are solely responsible for this.

The distinctive schism, which is noticeable in Dürer's work (cf. Wölfflin), characterizes the situation in which German art finds itself during the 16th century. Of the many great figures on the tomb of Maximilian in the *Hofkirche* at Innsbruck, the two most outstanding – masterly creations of Peter Vischer – are purely Renaissance. The statues are completely organic. They hardly copy anything from the sculpture of the leading Italians as regards plastic content. But the grille enclosing the tomb, finished about 1570, is still completely a creation of late Gothic linear feeling on a calligraphic basis. In particular those forms of curvingly bent and pierced round bars, which developed from the motif of a figure 8 and which make up the centre of the inner section these are directly calligraphic. With all the Renaissance serenity of the spiral panelling, the dynamism of the late Gothic imagination somehow finds expression. The tendril motif with vegetable details – vine leaves and other types of foliage – is again given expression. With the so-called 'branch-Gothic' a last refined development of the round bar has been discovered.

In other prominent examples the inner terminations of the long extended spiral motifs are fashioned with 'spindle-flowers.' The latter, comparable perhaps to the spiralling of a corkscrew, are formed on a wooden mold, which is then burnt. This method was also followed in the production of many other wrought-iron embellishments, especially in Spain. The grille is first put on to wood as a mounting. The wooden support is then burnt and the grille remains proof of how closely related mounting and grill-work are technically.

The spindle-flowers were an attempt to create a plastic effect with the round bar. In comparison to the Italian conception, however, all grille ornamentation which is developed from the round bar remains completely linear. Whatever might seem solid, reveals itself on closer inspection to be of pseudo-plastic make-up. The superficial character of the lattice-work is without a doubt maintained, no matter whether it is a case of abstract spiral motifs, pierced ironwork from a calligraphic pattern or similar to botanical details (leaves and tendrils). The illustrations in this book give some idea of the enormous wealth of 'rough' iron in this period.

A linear and superficial design is not the prerogative of German wrought-iron ornamentation of that time. Italy, France and Spain to a greater or lesser degree also participate. Linearity and superficiality belong to the technical and material foundations of the iron bar in general. Even Italy, despite her leading power in plastic formulations, was not able to escape these elementary conditions, and produced some excellent work through the media of pure features. But the characteristic calligraphic forms of northern imagination do not appear in the south. In place of the spiral, the S-scroll is predominant. Rather than the Gothic flamboyant panelling there is serene articulation of the surface in the Italian work. Even the space between the latticing, the 'hole,' has an important role to play. If this kind of grille was not actually architectonically designed, it seems static and tectonic in accordance with the artistic intentions of the southern way of thinking during the Renaissance.

Every Italian wrought-iron linear ornament made of round or flat bars (with the narrow edge occasionally turned towards the outside) appears comparatively widely spaced. It is surrounded by the 'hole' and by the air, as opposed to contemporary Gothic northern works. Not only spiral motifs, but also S- or C-scrolls are used in Germany as in Spain in such small sizes that everything seems narrowly spaced (cf.: grille, *Schloss Ambras*). Instead of the Italian clarity and lucidity which tends to bareness the Germans always offer bewildering profusion: panelling at all costs, as if because of a *horror vacui*.

The Spaniards yield a little to the Germans over this. The German and Spanish artistic spirit is synthesized

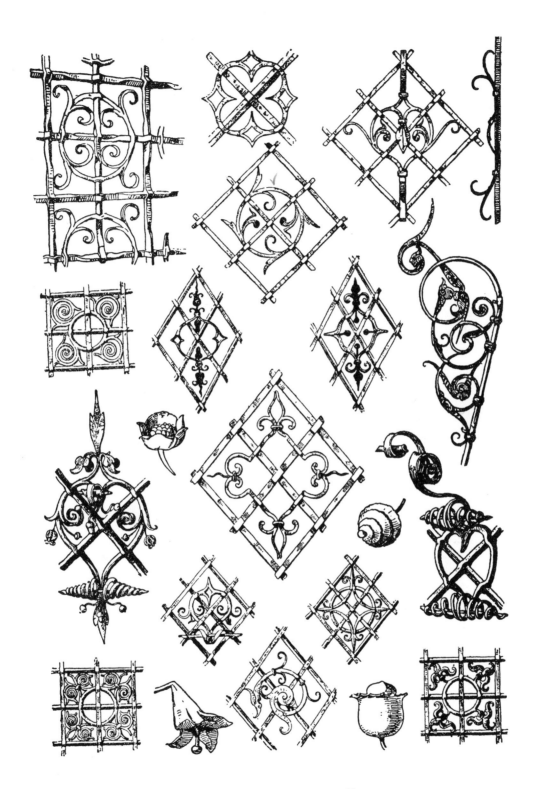

Details of German Renaissance grilles.

XXV

in the late Gothic and late Baroque styles. With the Spaniards an eastern influence comes into play. The striving after complete filling of the surface space has marked the oriental artistic temperament. The effect of some Spanish works in wrought iron, with their densely meshed pattern of curving ornamentation is similar in aesthetic character to an oriental carpet. Instead of the clarified simplicity, lucidity and stability of Italian forms, glittering, even punctulate effects come from the Spanish grilles. They surround in a close construction the extended choirs and the priests' seats, built far into the intersection of the nave and transepts and into the nave. They fence them off from the aisles and thus form reception rooms for the laity.

The oldest creative urges are present everywhere under the surface and determine the artistic result. The spirit of the Ancients, the humanistic law or anthropomorphic principle – man as the measure of all things – again and again came into view in Italian work. In the end this gained complete victory in the Renaissance period and reduced all decorative accessories and their ornamental treatment to absolute clarity. The simple and lucid form was at the same time the beautiful form, the 'great form' of classical art. Northern blood in Germany and oriental admixture in Spain made certain of a long-standing opposition to the classical make-up and to every rule of anthropomorphic thought in art, and constantly influenced German, French and Italian work.

The leading artists and craftsmen outside Italy could not evade the Italian and classical spirit. But France is much more responsible for the new movement in art, and is the true administrator of classical thought, especially in decorative wrought-iron work. Particularly, structural potentialities are seen in functional lattice-work.

The *grille d'honneur* becomes the main theme of decorative wrought iron. The plastic character, whose basic traits were already prepared by the Italians in the Renaissance period and developed in a special, way is strengthened. Yet instead of the cruder rusticity of the Italian structure, the French, and in their wake the Germans, now attain the most sophisticated effects in the service of a refined courtly and noble culture. The period of absolutism has come and with it Baroque, in its most distinguished worldly form, which is always influenced by classicism, especially in France.

XXVI

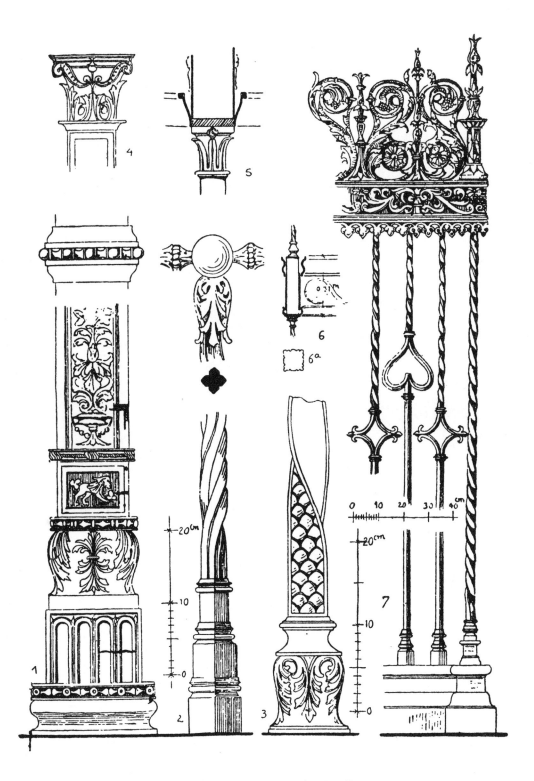

Spanish wrought-iron grilles. Details.

1. and 2. Cuenza cathedral, grille of the *Capilla major*, details from the lower section. 3., 4. and 5. Cuenza cathedral, parts of the grille behind the High Altar, by Sanchos Muñez. 6. Toledo cathedral, grille in the Chapel of the Holy Spirit, by Domingo Cespedes (1529), profile of frieze; 6a. Cross-section of the twisted bars. 7. Siguenza cathedral, chapel grille (1530).

Italian and French grilles, 16th century.

BAROQUE, ROCOCO AND CLASSICISM

France brings the deciding structural principle of the pure vertical arrangement made up of huge square bars (being the basic structure of the grille as well) to its final supremacy in the great grille. The rigid upright bars dispense with the frame round and through which the ornamental accessories can move, and complicate the design dynamically. But the strong and clear arrangement of the upright bars subordinates the ornamental form, which becomes confined to the upper part of the framework, which itself takes on a flamboyant shape. The calmness of the structure and the flamboyance of the framework are perfectly synthesized.

Architectonics retain the lead in the same way that, in functional architecture, all décor must finally submit to structure, but above all to space. Under the architectural rule of the Baroque – a style unequalled for its use of space – the grille-work becomes a frame for space. The function of the grille and its ornamental forms in the service of architecture is to preserve and produce space. All the means of advanced illusionist perspective are used in the linear bar work of the grille to create a deeper impression of space. Undisputedly the highest achievements of the Baroque period are to be found here, and especially in the German work of the 18th century.

Appreciation of the Baroque and Rococo periods has, since the classical period in literature under the leadership of Johann Joachim Winckelmann and a correspondingly attuned written history of art and aesthetics, varied greatly. However, connoisseurs have always appreciated the achievements of the smiths and locksmiths. Adolf Menzel, particularly, noted the artistic charm of grilles from the Baroque and Rococo periods. He could not do enough faithfully to imitate in his paintings the partly barren, partly flamboyant forms of decorative wrought iron work.

The simple structure of the square upright sections is the basis for the many ornamental complications in the grille-work of the Baroque and Rococo periods. These sections form the lower part and take the lead.

They are intertwined with tendrils and twisting straps which partly remain abstractly material and which are partly transformed into plant motifs. In a relatively early example of French wrought-iron work this is especially clear and even rather crudely executed (cf. illustration: p. 126). The upright system of square bars suggests the basic idea. The bars are quite widely spaced. Curving flat irons produce the horizontal support in the middle and the top. In between these it branches out upwards and to the sides. A formal vine with leaves and shoots – the last after-effects of the old late Gothic spindle-flowers – is woven into the inflexible framework of branches made by the upright bars. In this way, they have attempted to call from the grille a lively flamboyant effect. Even if the whole thing still remains a little barren, that is because it is founded in a comparatively early stage (compared with the coming achievements). This is not the highest achievement, although the basic division into structural and flamboyant parts in the handling of the inner section definitely prevails.

The great and first-rate works show a much greater wealth of motifs. They are no longer just linear, but completely plastic in execution. Nevertheless, the rigid basic structure is always paramount. In a magnificent example of the new style which is also the great style of the French 17th century – of the *grand siècle* – this seems to have developed to the highest perfection in the magnificent portal grilles from the *château Maison-Lafitte*, now in the Louvre in Paris.

This palace was the masterpiece of François Mansart and was built for Monsieur de Longueil. The grilles are really worthy of the architecture. A rigid framework of wide fillets holds everything together. In the frame itself interlacing circular figures produce a structurally serene filling interspersed at certain points (at the foot, in the middle and at the upper corners) with lions' heads like the old bronze door mountings. The surfaces of both wings of the gate are also surrounded with a narrow border-strap with circular motifs and in the vertical middle line they are divided by the same straps. The exact middle of each wing is bordered by an oval. In this actual inner section, surrounded and made smaller in this way, is housed a plastically perfected wrought-iron ornament. Vegetable motifs, like rolled-up acanthus leaves with rosettes, form S-scrolls. The ensuing plastic spirals end high above with birds' heads. A classically designed cornice produces the upper termination. Between this framework it once again develops into an unrivalled wealth of ornamental infilling. From a central grotesque figure, a masculine form, flanked by two figures of children holding a crown, spiral motifs run to both sides and fill the side sections densely with their massive clustered solidity. The design of the so-called foliage work – so well loved in stucco during the second half of the 17th century – has reached the highest stage in iron. This is an extreme example of what wrought iron can do; thoroughly Baroque, it conforms to the kind of décor which is well loved in France by Le Brun. Classical superficiality in the apportionment and framing, baroque plasticity in the panelling, are brought together in a unique synthesis.

This marks the general situation of artistic creativeness in France's great century, that is in the age of Louis XIV. The pompous decoration develops in the structural casing of classical simplicity. In contrast to the decorative imagination of a Le Brun, we have the French architectural classics in masonry of Charles Perrault (Louvre colonnade) and Jules Hardouin Mansart (completion of Versailles, dome of *Les Invalides* and other such work).

In a second portal from *Maison-Lafitte* the sterner, academic and classical spirit is more prevalent. In place of the high plastic panelling of the leaves of the door with foliage and tendril-like coils in the shape of an S, the whole panel, with the exception of the oval middle sections, is now closely intertwined with framework motifs. Just the remaining narrow upright sections are accentuated by a kind of extended baluster pillar. Serene surface apportionment and framing, in the classical sense, prevails. The cresting on this second portal is like that of the first magnificent gate in the elevated plasticity of its ornamental panelling.

The luxury of wrought iron is further increased in the great grilles with which the forecourts of the French palaces and *hôtels* (dwellings of nobility) are enclosed, made secure and at the same time decora-

tively accentuated. Here, in the *grille d'honneur*, is the most masterly treatment of iron.

The grille was immediately related to the structure of the outer area. Since it has to fulfill a space-preserving function, it is a piece of façade as well, and must obey structural laws. The architectonic principle is victorious over the decorative. The section made up of square upright bars, decorated with spikes and tassels at the top, determines the total impression. Above the portals, which are vaulted with cornices, jutting out sometimes sparsely, sometimes densely, rich ornamentation is again used: royal and noble insignias surrounded by plastically executed vegetable embellishments. Flamboyance is only in the cresting. The impression of static serenity in the upright bars of the inner section is predominant.

The superbly majestic grilles from Versailles may have once set the fashion, like the whole layout of this *château* and park for which Jules Hardouin Mansart and the genius of spacious landscape gardening, André Lenôtre, are responsible.

Although structurally rigid, these large grilles are fully spacious. Through the ironwork a separate court or a series of courts are framed. Originally superficial and two-dimensional, it is now three-dimensional. The stages of pure linearity and plastic conception have borne fruit. Thus the circle of higher artistic potentialities in the use of wrought iron is complete.

That which was wrought in the time of Louis XIV into stronger academic and classical bonds now freely develops in the coming Regency period and then in the Rococo period (Louis XV). The greatest achievement of this epoch is the famous grille round the *Place Stanislas* in Nancy, by Jean Lamour, the court smith to King Stanislas Leszcynski. The bars and compound bars terminate at striking and structurally important points in formal pillars and pilasters, resembling contemporary trellis work. Trellis work of wood and grille-work of iron must serve the higher aim, which was alone near to the heart of the creative idea of that period: adaptation to architectural planning. The municipal planning of the beautiful square in Nancy is solved with a finality which has no equal anywhere. If, as A. E. Brinckmann says, town planning means producing space by using houses, then the work of the smiths in Nancy conforms completely to the idea in this sentence and therefore meets the highest artistic demands. The grilles of Jean Lamour

Venetian grilles, 16th to 18th century

are most notable for the exemplary solution to town planning which is prevalent in the creation of the famous series of squares in Nancy.

Besides, the grille-work surrounding the square contains a charming antithesis. It encloses the actual space, yet allows the unbounded vastness of space in the countryside to stream in everywhere through its bars and meshes. This is quite in keeping with late Baroque thought: the building is spaced out, so that an abundance of light and air may come in: architectural planning *en plein air*.

In the large portal-like openings in the Stanislas grille, decorative groups of figurative plasticity are placed: fountains send their rushing streams of water into widely protruding basins, the grilles themselves follow the form of the square in a curve, its course

gives the corners a good rounding-off. All methods of a contrapuntal style, producing space, changing from concave to convex, are developed as in the façades of other buildings of the late Baroque and Rococo.

Above the rigid upright division of the grilles there is an unending profusion of flamboyant *rocaille* motifs which, wrought and formed here in iron, is equal to the best workmanship of the sculptors and stucco workers. High above the powerful cornices, the imagination explodes into the air with flamboyant details, without, at the same time ignoring the functional movement. Germany first put into practice the final consequences in the simple and airy treatment of the upper frame of such grilles (cf. Würzburg etc.). On the Stanislas grille in Nancy the

XXXI

synthesis of rigidity and flamboyance, from the stability of the upright bars and the instability of the ornamental trimmings has in every case succeeded completely. French taste has found fulfillment.

Soon enough there remains from the ornamental ecstasy of the *rocaille* imagination only the rigid frame of the uprights. Heavy form triumphs over the light. The basic classical mood breaks through and gives the *grille d'honneur* in the great forecourts of the monumental buildings a new dignity which from now on seems timely. The phases of late Baroque classicism are given. The *style Louis XVI* is here. The dynamically complicated form of the accessories disappears. The great compound form of strong structural make-up asserts itself. The curves are turned into edges and corners. The spiral becomes stiffened into a meander *à la grecque*. In the frame we find simple circular motifs again like the heavy doors of the *château* of *Maison-Lafitte*. *Grand style* and Louis XVI style are similar in their formal bearing.

The sides of the portals are mighty pillars made of square bars. Starkly profiled cornices bear down heavily over the wings of the gates. But above the whole width of the grilles there is spread a single long row of pointed spikes decorated with tassels. The grille distributes distanced refinement: an unmerciful exclusiveness lies in this effect created by typical French grilles. The surroundings of the courts in the *Palais de Justice* or of the *École militaire* in Paris are of this type – the final achievements of self-sufficient decorative wrought iron outside Germany.

In opposition to the marvellous grille in Nancy the Germans have produced the overwhelming work of the outer grille for the forecourt of the *Residenz-schloss* in Würzburg. The grille was a curving barrier, both concave and convex, broken by many corners. Stone pillars and sentry boxes with obelisks produced the necessary supports and stresses. In the grille itself the upright framework of bars receded before the flamboyant character of the ornamental accessories. And here above all the upper frame was set free in *rocaille* motifs which seem spontaneously poised.

All that *rocaille* imagination had ever designed found its place on the arched cornices of the garden gates at Würzburg. The flamboyance has completely played itself out in the framework, like that wreath of colored stucco ornaments, which were fixed to the shallow hollows of the festive church interiors, here

Wrought-iron gate in Salisbury, 18th century

Rococo grilles from Germany, France and Italy.

as there serving as frames for a three-dimensional creation.

A few degrees lighter than the Würzburg grille is the famous chancel grille in the abbey church of Amorbach. Fineness has replaced plastic magnificence, as if to prove that wrought-iron work is really the practical embodiment of a linear idea.

In order that the law of absolute unity of space and accessories is completely fulfilled, a more advanced fashioning of the iron lines of the grille takes control to produce unique effects in perspective. The positioning of the bars brings out the illusion of great depth. The intensification of the dimension of depth is complete. Examples of this are the chancel grille in *Weingarten*, in *Zwiefalten* and in the Swiss *Wall-fahrtskirche Maria Einsiedeln*. The central section of the famous chancel grille in Zwiefalten creates a formal surrounding to the altar with a construction in perspective, that is, with the illusion of depth, round the Virgin Mary and the Christ Child in radiant glory. The limit is reached. The smiths have done justice fully to the demands for a style in three-dimensional flamboyance.

What follows ends with the triviality of cast iron, apart from some reproductions of French style of the Louis XVI period. The needs of the time lower all creative forces to the dark continent of romanticism. These buried seeds have not yet produced any new blooms. But in the harsher reality of a technical period wrought-iron now comes under another law!

XXXIII

NOTE ON ILLUSTRATIONS

Acknowledgement is made to the following individuals and institutions for photographs used in the plates:

Alinari, Florence: pages 22, 23, 24, 31, 43, 63, 64, 67, 68, 69, 86, 87, 92, 93, 97, 98, 99. Brogi, Florence: page 21. Giroudon, A., Paris: pages 7, 18, 126, 137, 185, 216, 312. Laurent y Cia, Madrid: pages 2, 3, 74, 75, 76, 77, 78, 79, 80, 81, 82, 83, 84, 85. Moscione, Rome: pages 96, 180. Müller, Christof, Nürnberg: pages 44, 47, 102, 108, 116, 131. Österreichische Lichtbildstelle, Vienna 1: pages 27, 28, 29, 34, 54, 57, 107, 152, 153, 156, 157, 158, 159, 175, 220, 221, 222, 223, 224, 225, 231, 232, 233, 234, 235, 236, 237, 244, 245, 246, 254, 279, 280, 281, 285, 286, 304, 311, 316. Poppi, Bologne: page 306. Reusch, August, Munich: pages 36, 38, 39, 40, 41, 48, 53, 111, 150, 154, 174, 252, 253, 255, 283, 304. From: H. R. d'Allemagne, Ferronnerie ancienne, Paris 1924: pages 5, 6, 31, 95, 190. From: Contet, F., Documents de Ferronnerie ancienne, Paris 1922: page 1.

THE PLATES

France, 12th century. Detail of grille in Le Puy Cathedral

Spain, 12th century. Iron mounted door in the abbey, Marcevols (Northern Spain)

Spain, 13th century. Wrought-iron door in Palencia cathedral

4

France, 13th century. Grille from the abbey, Ourscamp,
now in the Musée Le Secq des Tournelles, Rouen

France, 13th century. Detail of grille from the abbey, Ourscamp

6

France, 13th century. Fire-screen in the Musée Le Secq des Tournelles, Rouen

France, 13th century. Wrought-iron grilles embellishment, Musée des Arts Décoratifs, Paris

France, 13th century. 1) and 3) Grilles, Musée de Cluny, Paris; 2) Door-mounting, Victoria and Albert Museum, London

France, second half of 13th century. Iron mounted chest. Victoria and Albert Museum, London

10

Liège, 13th century. Door, formerly in the Church of St. Paul, now in the Museum, Liège

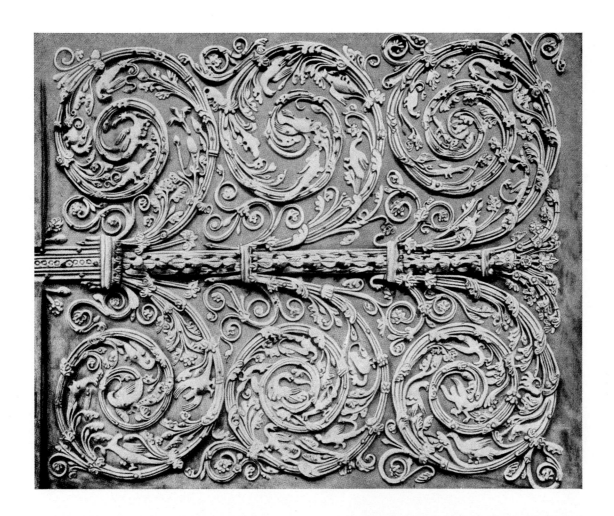

France, 13th century. Door-mountings: 1) Notre Dame, Paris; 2) Cathedral, Saint Gilles

France, 13th century. Iron mounted door on the west front of the cathedral, Paris

Germany, first half of 14th century. The cathedral door, Erfurt

14

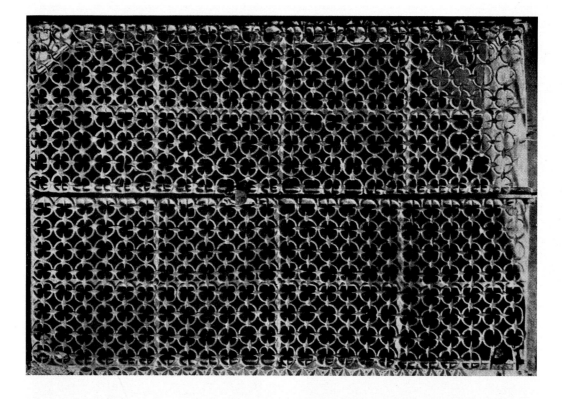

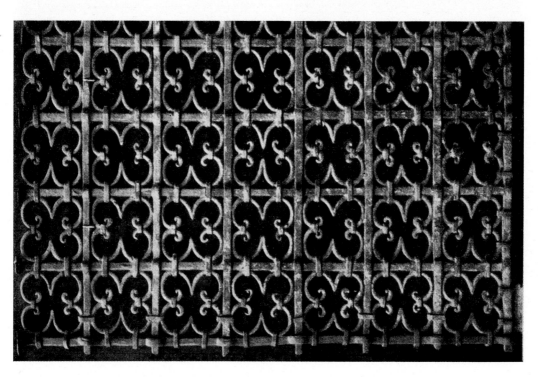

Grilles. 1) France, 13th century; 2) Italy, early 14th century

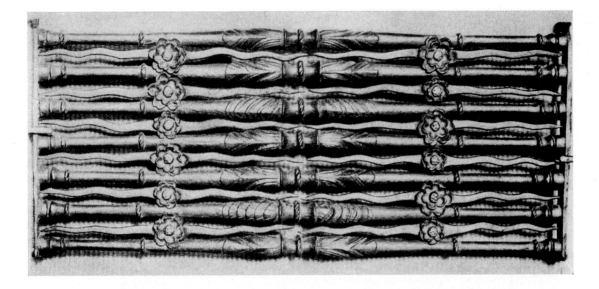

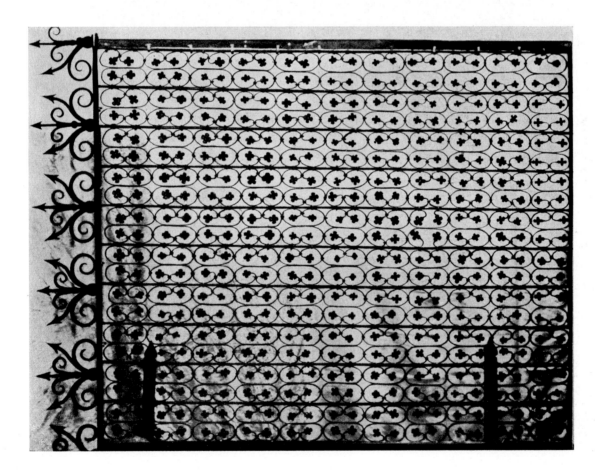

Grille from Lüneburg, 13th to 14th century; 2) France, 13th century

16

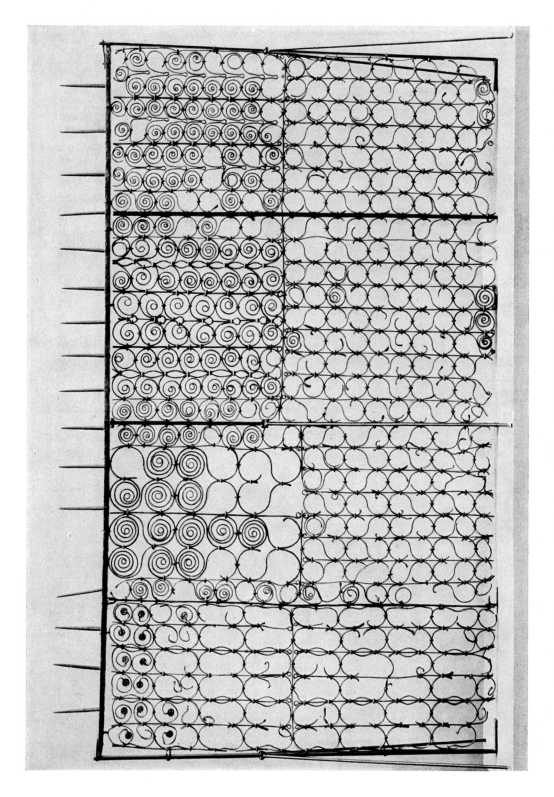

England, 13th century. Grille from Chichester Cathedral. Victoria and Albert Museum, London

England, 14th to 15th century. Grille in the Victoria and Albert Museum, London

18

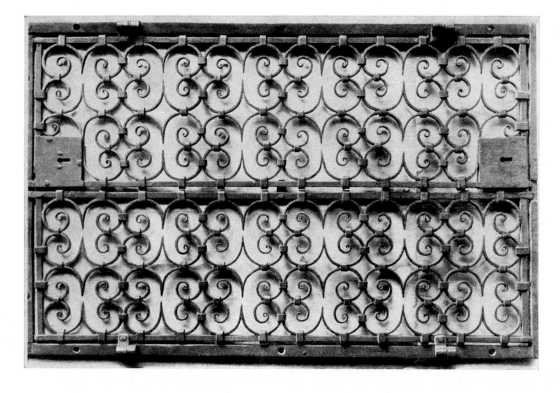

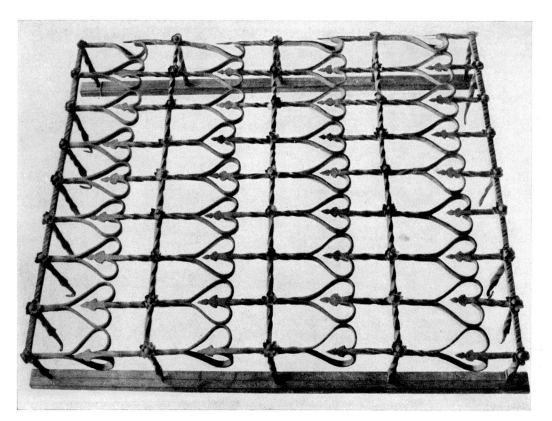

France, 1) Window-grille from Bourges, 14th century; 2) Grille, 15th century, in the Musée des Arts Décoratifs, Paris

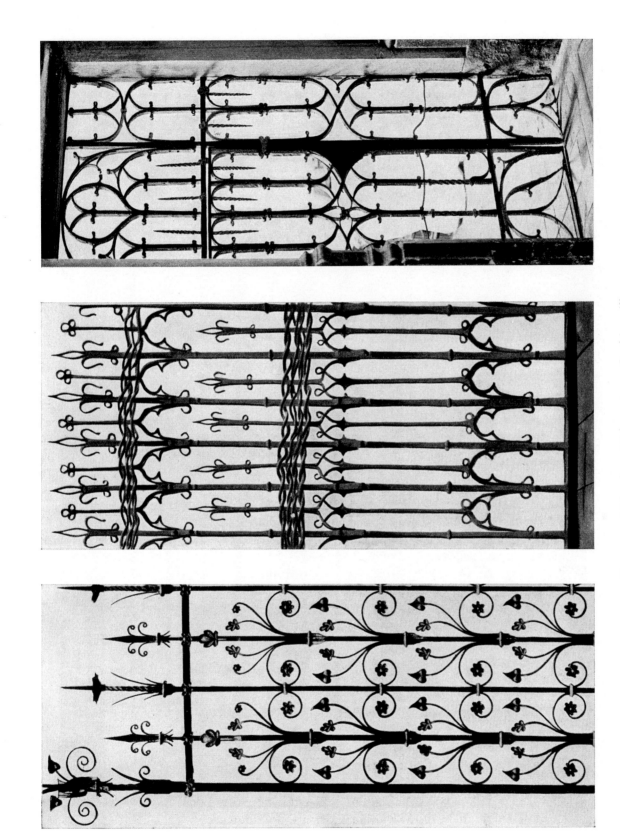

France and Flanders, 15th century. Gothic grilles

Italy, c. 1370. Grille in Santa Croce, Florence

Italy, c. 1380. Grille on the tomb of the Scaligers in Verona

Italy, c. 1400. Grille in the Palazzo Pubblico, Siena

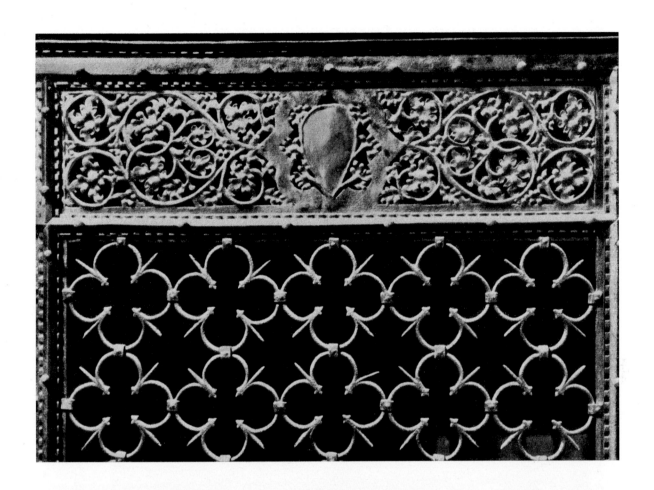

Italy. 1) Grille, c. 1400, in Santa Trinità, Florence;
2) Iron casket, Siena, 15th century

24

Grille and door with metal filigree-panelling, 1) Florence, 14th century; 2) Austria, 15th century

Guichet and tabernacle door, Austria, 15th century

26

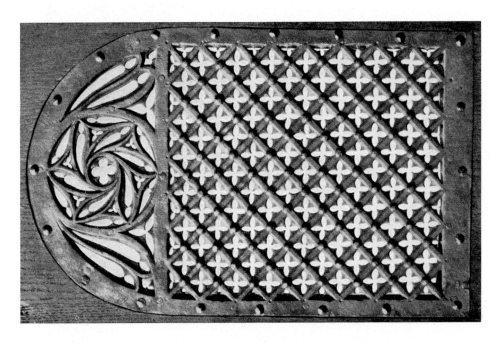

Germany, 15th century. Guichets, Museum für Kunst und Gewerbe, Hamburg

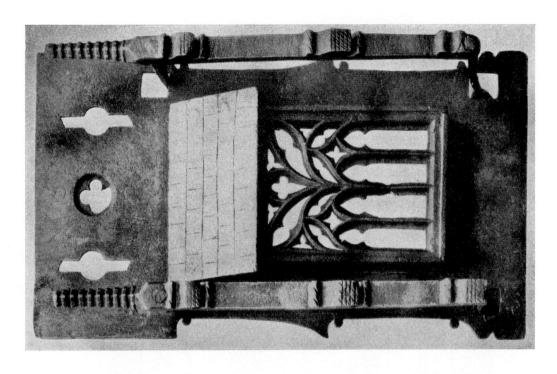

Left: Tabernacle door, Austria, 15th century. Right: Guichet, France, 15th century

Austria, 15th century. Tabernacle door in the infirmary church, Krems

Austria, 15th century. Tabernacle door in the infirmary church, Krems

Netherlands, 15th century. Guichet, Victoria and Albert Museum, London

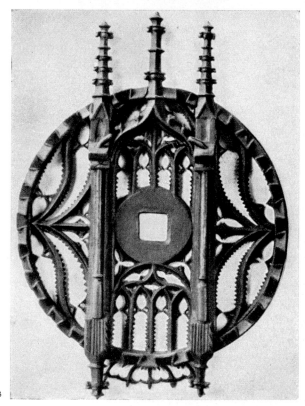

1) and 4) Guichets, France, 15th century; 2) Tabernacle door, Netherlands,
15th century; 3) Part of a door-knocker, France, 15th century

Details of tabernacle and sacristy doors, Austria, 15th century

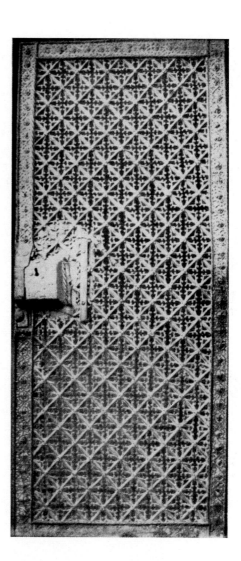

Germany, late 15th century. Wrought-iron doors and window-grilles

Austria, 15th century. Door of the Maria-Stiegenkirche, Vienna

Hungary, 15th century. Door in the church at Lápis-Patak

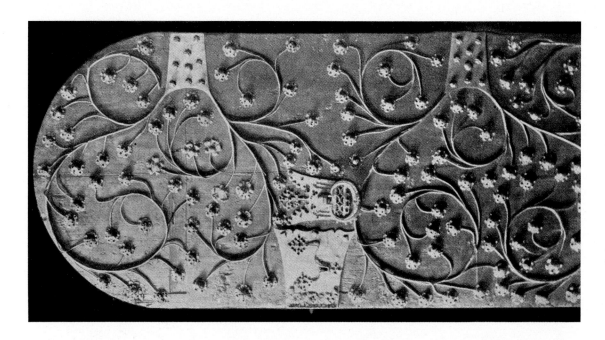

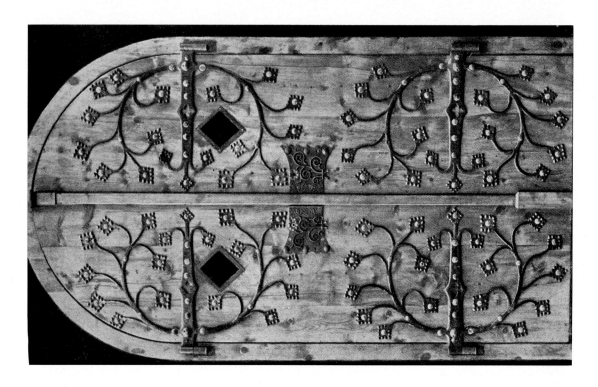

South Germany, 15th century. Iron mounted doors

Germany, 15th century. Iron mounted doors. Germanisches Museum, Nuremberg

South Germany, 15th century. Iron mounted doors

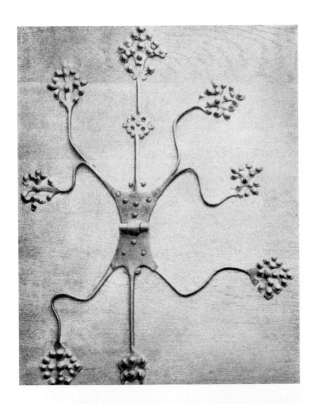

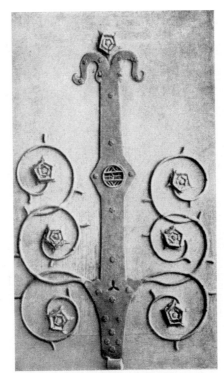

South Germany, 15th century. Door-mountings

South Germany, 15th century. Door-mounting

South Germany, 15th century. Door-mounting

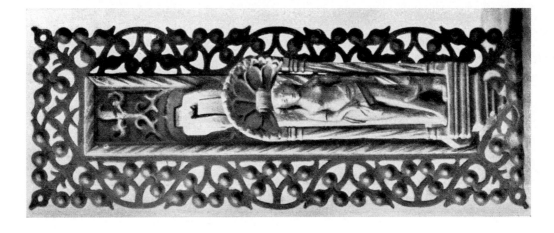

France, 15th century. Lock scutcheons, Musée de Cluny, Paris

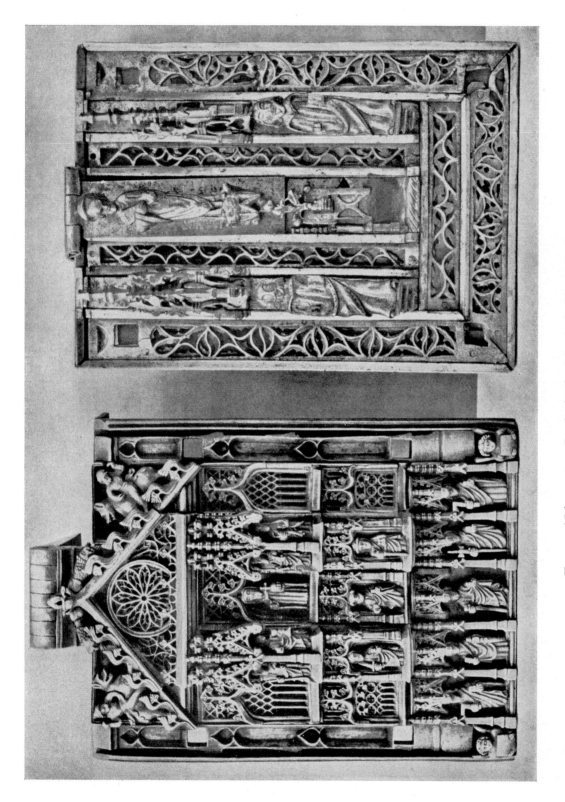

France, 15th century. Locks in the Musée de Cluny, Paris

Germany, end of 15th century. Lock mountings. Germanisches Museum, Nuremberg

Germany, 1450–1500. Door-knockers and mountings in the Bayerisches Nationalmuseum, Munich

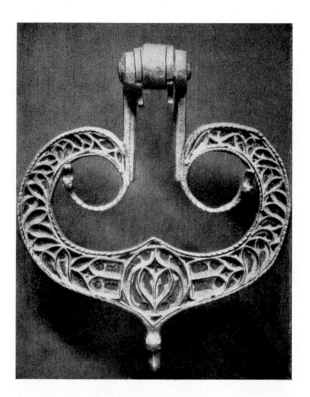

Germany, 15th century. Door-knockers

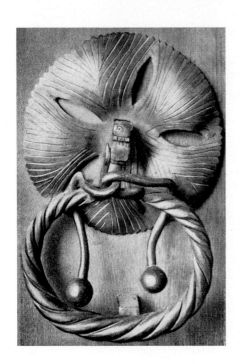

Germany, 15th century. Door-handle and door-knockers

South Germany, 16th century. Iron mounted door

Germany, 16th century. Iron mounted door. Nuremberg craftsmanship

Switzerland, 15th century. Door-handles in the Historisches Museum, Basle

Switzerland, 15th century. Door-handles, Historisches Museum, Basle

Germany, 15th century. Scutcheon for a door-handle,
Nuremberg, Germanisches Museum

South Germany, c. 1500. Wrought-iron tabernacle,
Bayerisches Nationalmuseum, Munich

54

Tyrol, c. 1500. Grille in the parish church, Hall

Germany, c. 1470. Grille in St. Ulrichskirche, Augsburg

Tyrol, c. 1500. Grille in the parish church, Hall

Tyrol, c. 1500. Grille in the parish church, Hall

North Brabant, Burg Heeswyk, 15th century. Chandelier

Germany, 15th century. Chandelier, Nationalmuseum, Munich

Germany. Late Gothic bracket from the church at Zülpich (Rhineland)

Germany, late 15th century. Bracket in the Kunstgewerbe-Museum, Cologne

62

Germany, beginning of 16th century. Branched candlestick, St. Johanniskirche, Cologne

Italy, 15th century. Wrought-iron fire-place tools (andirons). Museum, Turin

France, 15th century. 1) Door-knocker, 2) Grille, French craftsmanship, in the Museo Nazionale, Florence

Spain, 16th century. Fire-screen in the Louvre, Paris

Spain, 1525. Pulpit in the cathedral, Avila

Italy, 15th century. Lantern in the Palazzo Guadagni, Florence

Italy, 15th century. Torch holders. Left: in the Palazzo Grisoli, Florence, right: in the Piazza Postierla, Siena

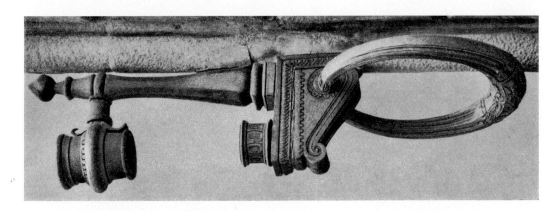

Italy, 15th century. Standard holders in Florentine places

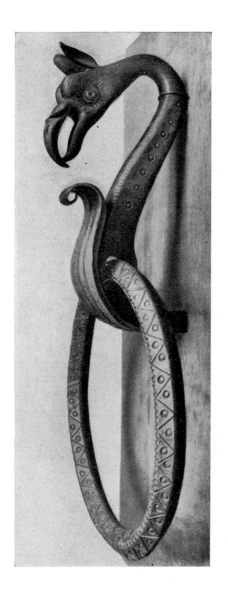

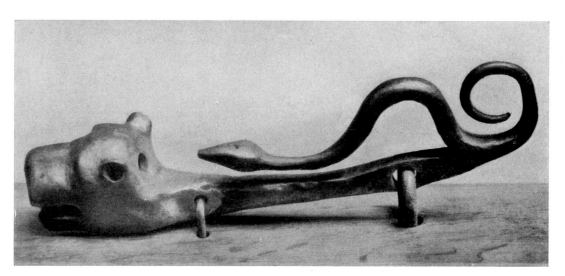

Door-knockers from Italy, 15th and 16th century. Schlossmuseum, Berlin

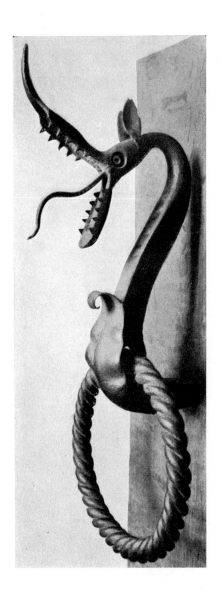

Door-knockers from Italy, 15th and 16th century. Schlossmuseum, Berlin

72

Italy, c. 1500. Grille in the Palazzo Bevilaqua, Bologna

Italy, c. 1500. Balcony railing in the Palazzo Bevilaqua, Bologna

Spain, 15th century. Grille in Barcelona cathedral

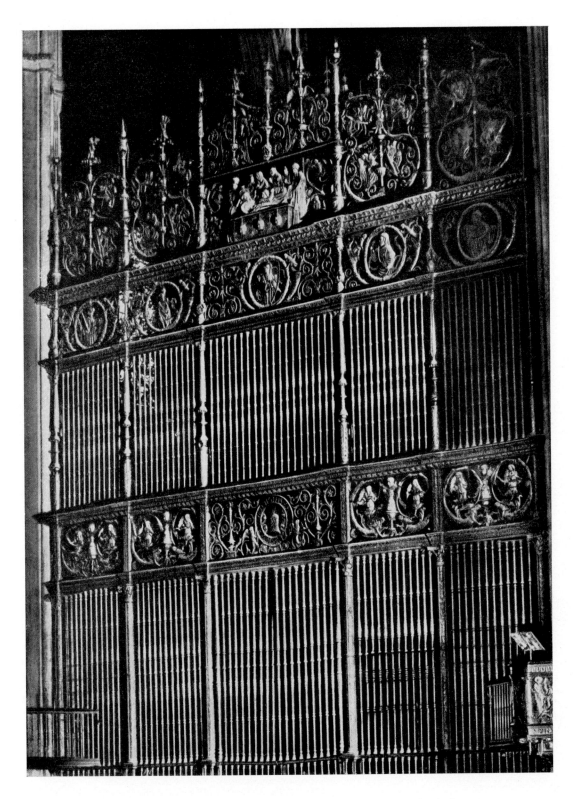

Spain, c. 1530. Grille in Capilla Mayor, Seville Cathedral

Spain, 16th century. Grille in Plasencia cathedral

Spain, 16th century. Screen in Saragosa

Spain, 16th century. Screen in Jerez de la Frontera

Spain, 16th century. Grille of the royal chapel in the cathedral, Granada

Spain, 16th century. Window grille in Salamanca

Spain, 16th century. Window grille in Salamanca

Spain, 16th century. Window grille in Seville

Spain, c. 1560. Wrought-iron grille

Spain, 16th century. Chapel screen in Palencia cathedral

Spain, 16th century. Grille in Salamanca University

Venice, Scuola di S. Giorgio. Window grille, end of 15th century

Italy, 15th century. Details of window grilles from Venice

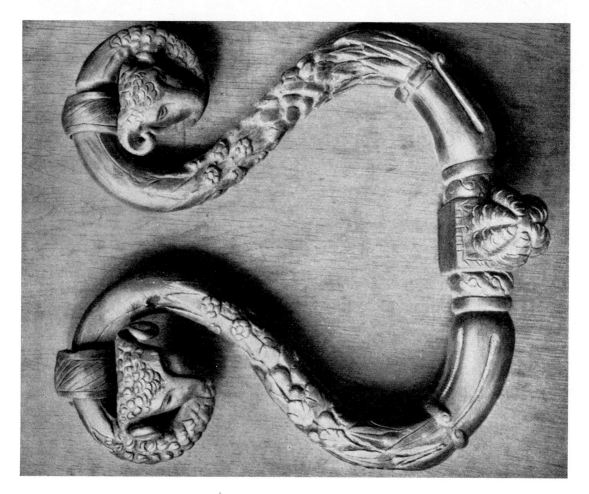

Italy, 16th century. Door-knockers in the Schlossmuseum, Berlin

Door-knockers, 16th century. Right: France, Musée de Cluny, Paris; left: Italy, Schlossmuseum, Berlin

France, 16th century. Grille in Rouen

France, 16th century. Iron gate in Le Mans

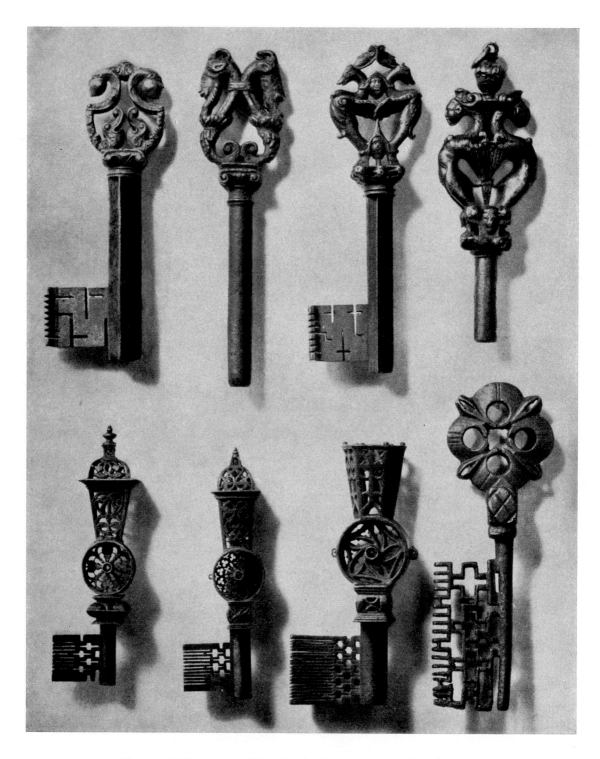

France, 16th century. Keys in the Museo Nazionale, Florence

France, 16th century. Door-handle and door-knockers, Museo Nazionale, Florence

94

Italy, 16th century. Grilles in the Schlossmuseum, Berlin

Italy, 16th century. Window grille in the Musée Le Secq des Tournelles, Rouen

Italy, 16th century. Grille, Chiesa di S. Marco, Rome

Italy, 16th century. Fanlight grilles from Lucca

Northern Italy, 16th century. Wrought-iron door

Northern Italy, 16th century. Grille in the cathedral, Trieste

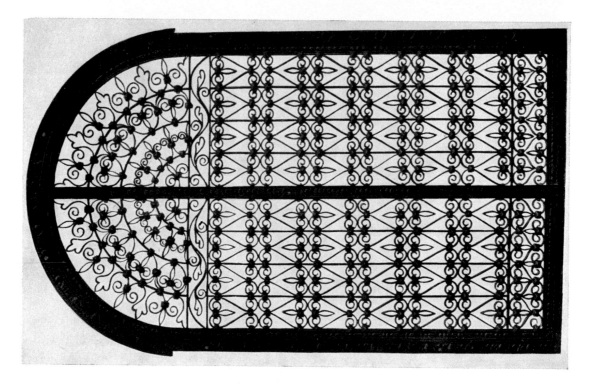

Northern Italy, 16th century. Grilles in the Schlossmuseum, Berlin

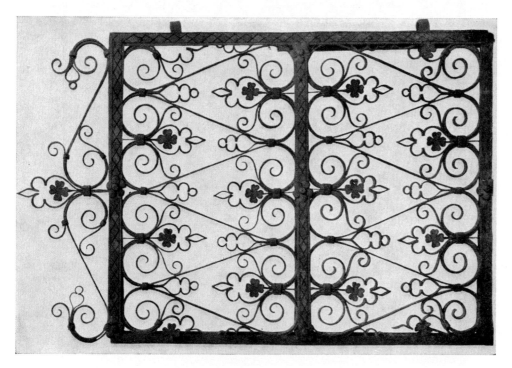

Northern Italy, end of 16th century. Grilles in the Schlossmuseum, Berlin

102

Germany, 16th century. Wrought-iron door, Germanisches Museum, Nuremberg

Germany, 16th century. 1) Fanlight grille, Nuremberg
2) Window grille in the Victoria and Albert Museum, London

Germany, end of 16th century. Fanlight grille and window decoration

Germany, 16th century. Grilles from the cathedral, Brunswick

Austria, c. 1570. Wrought-iron door in Schloss Ambras (Tyrol)

Austria, c. 1570. Well canopy in Schloss Grafenegg

Germany, end of 16th century. Grilles in the Germanisches Museum, Nuremberg

Germany, c. 1580. Grille in the St. Ulrichskirche, Augsburg

Germany, c. 1580. Grille in the St. Ulrichskirche, Augsburg

South Germany, end of 16th century. Detail of a screen

112

Iron mounted door in Pressburg. 16th century

Germany, 16th to 17th century. Wrought-iron door from Augsburg

Fanlight grille and window grating from Freiberg (Saxony)

Germany, end of 16th century. Window grille from Zittau (Saxony)

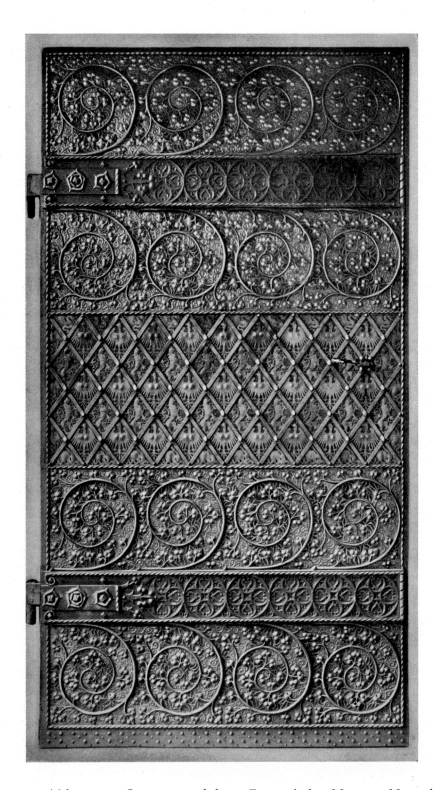

Germany, 16th century. Iron mounted door, Germanisches Museum, Nuremberg

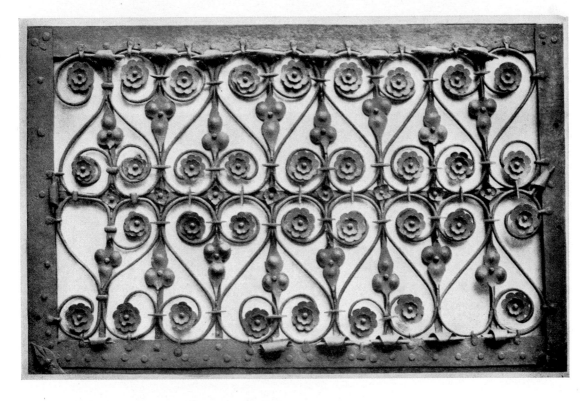

Door panels: 1) Germany, mid-16th century; 2) Austria, 16th to 17th century

118

Germany, 16th to 17th century. Door-knockers, Schlossmuseum, Berlin

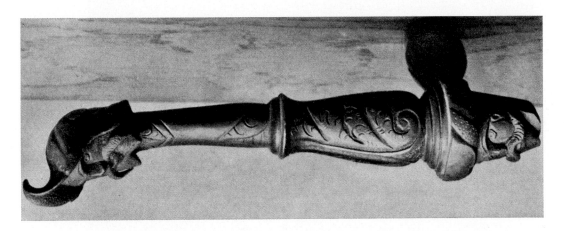

Germany, 16th century. Door-knockers and door-handle, Schlossmuseum, Berlin

Germany, 16th century. Door-knockers, Schlossmuseum, Berlin

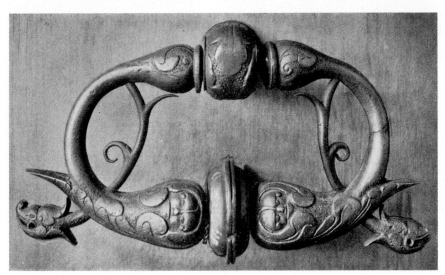

Germany, 16th century. Door-knockers, Schlossmuseum, Berlin

Germany, 16th century. Door-knockers in the Schlossmuseum, Berlin

Germany, 16th to 17th century. Door-knockers in the Schlossmuseum, Berlin

124

Germany, c. 1595. Grille in Freiberg cathedral (Saxony)

Germany, c. 1677. Iron screen in the Peterskirche, Görlitz

France, 16th century. Wrought-iron gate, Château de Blois

Brackets, 16th century. 1) in Bruges (Flanders); 2) Germany

Germany, wrought iron work of the end of 16th century and beginning of 17th century

Italy, 17th century. Tabernacle doors:: 1) Schlossmuseum, Berlin;
2) Victoria and Albert Museum, Berlin

130

Germany, end of 17th century. Grille in Breslau

Germany, 17th century. Grille in the Germanisches Museum, Nuremberg

Germany, 17th century. Grilles from Augsburg and Breslau

France, end of 16th century. Grille in the Musée Carnavalet, Paris

134

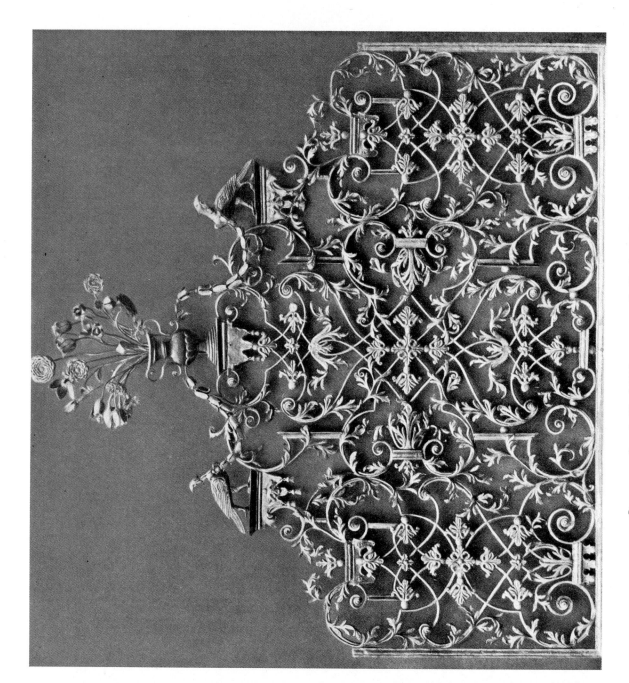

Germany, first half of 17th century. Grille from Dresden

Germany, 1637. Grille in the Kunstgewerbemuseum, Dresden

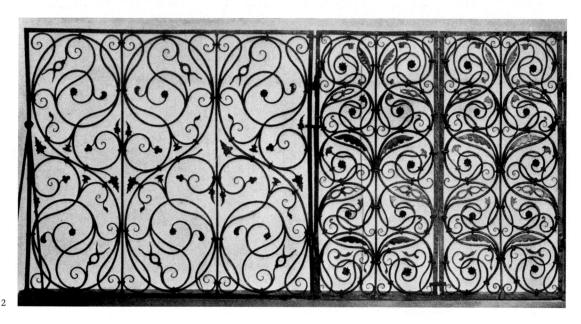

South Germany, mid-17th century. 1) Grille in Munich;
2) Detail of a grille in the Victoria and Albert Museum, London

Denmark, beginning of 17th century. Chapel grille in the cathedral, Roeskilde

140

Denmark, 17th century. Chapel grille in the cathedral, Roeskilde

Denmark, 17th century. Grille in Oxholm (Jutland)

Denmark, c. 1650. Chapel screen in the cathedral, Ripen

Germany, c. 1668. Well canopy in Neisse (Silesia)

Germany, c. 1630. Wrought-iron well enclosure in Danzig

Germany, 17th century. 1) Grille from Danzig, c. 1620;
2) from Görlitz, end of 17th century

South Germany and Austria, early 17th century. Grilles

South Germany and Northern Italy, 17th century. Grilles in the Schlossmuseum, Berlin

148

South Germany, mid-17th century. Window grilles

South Germany, second half of 17th century. Window grilles

South Germany, first half of 17th century. Grilles from Augsburg and Freiburg

Wrought-iron work from South Germany and Hungary, end of 17th century

Austria, second half of 17th century. Screen in the cathedral church of Graz

Prague, second half of 17th century. Screen in the Salvator church

154

South Germany, 17th century. Detail of a church grille

Germany, c. 1700. Grilles in Lübeck, Marienkirche

156

Prague, mid-17th century. Grille in the church of St. George

157

Prague, second half of 17th century. Grilles in the Collegium Clementinum

Prague, second half of 17th century. Grille in the Italian Chapel

Prague, second half of 17th century. Grille in the Collegium Clementinum

160

Germany, end of 17th century. Fanlight grille from Vienna;
Window grille from Görlitz

Northern Italy, end of 17th century. Fanlight grille and balcony railing

Germany, second half of 17th century. Wrought-iron doors in Schleswig cathedral

Germany, second half of 17th century. Wrought-iron door in Schleswig cathedral

Germany, end of 17th century. Grille in Augsburg cathedral

Germany, c. 1698. Wrought-iron doors in St. Ulrichskirche, Augsburg

Denmark, c. 1700. Middle section of the chapel grille in the cathedral, Roeskilde

Denmark, c. 1700. Chapel grille in the cathedral, Roeskilde

Germany, c. 1700. Framed grille in the Gewerbemuseum, Nuremberg

South Germany, beginning of 18th century. Grille, St. Emeranskirche, Regensburg

Germany, second half of 17th century. Grilles, Germanisches Museum, Nuremberg

Germany, beginning of 18th century. Fanlight grilles

Germany, early 18th century. Grille from Cologne, in the Victoria and Albert Museum, London

South Germany, c. 1726. Detail of a wrought-iron door in Regensburg

South Germany, beginning of 17th century. Grave-crosses

South Germany, second half of 17th century. Grave-crosses

Italy, 17th century. Window grilles: 1) Schlossmuseum Berlin;
2) Victoria and Albert Museum, London

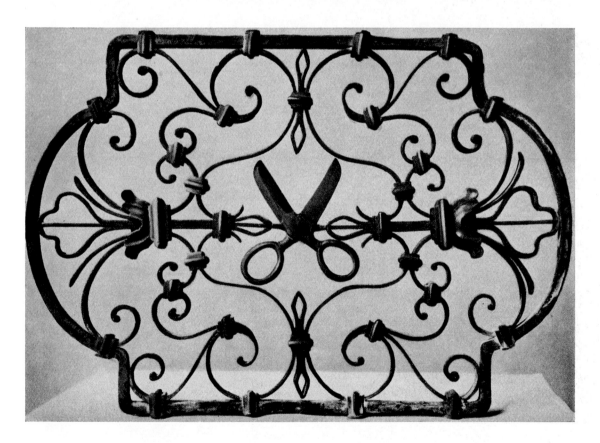

Italy, 17th century. Window grilles: 1) Schlossmuseum, Berlin;
2) Museum für Kunst und Gewerbe, Hamburg

178

Northern.Italy, 17th century. Window grilles, 1) Victoria and Albert Museum, London; 2) Schlossmuseum, Berlin

Italy, 17th century. Grille, Victoria and Albert Museum, London

Italy, 17th century. Grille in the Basilica of San Giovanni in Laterano, Rome

France, 17th century. Wrought-iron gates in the Musée Carnavalet, Paris

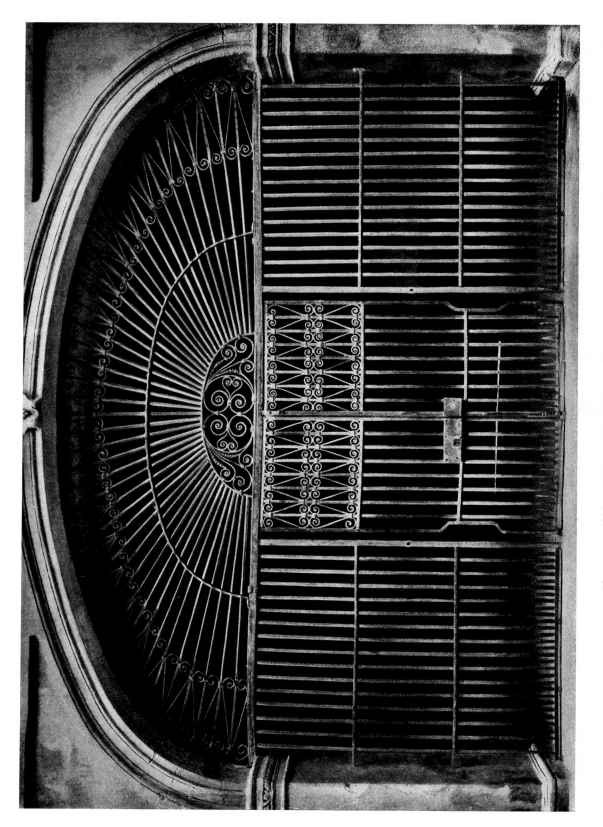

France, c. 1661. Grille in Hôtel de Ville, Aix-en-Provence

France, 17th century. 1) Grille in Marseille, Musée Borelli; 2) Grille in the Palace of Versailles

France, end of 17th century. Grilles in Convent de la Visitation, Lyons

France, 17th century. Wrought-iron gates in Aix-en-Provence

France, 17th century. Wrought-iron gates and railings in Jardin Botanique, Angers

France, c. 1680. Wrought-iron gates and railings in the forecourt of the Palace of Versailles

France, c. 1680. Detail of the railings in the forecourt of the Palace of Versailles

France, 17th century. Wrought-iron balustrade, Hotel Duchâtelet, Paris

France, end of 17th century. 1) Fanlight grille, Schlossmuseum, Berlin;
2) Window grille, Musée Le Secq des Tournelles, Rouen

France, 17th century. Window grille in the Musée de Cluny, Paris

France, early 18th century. Wrought-iron balustrade in Dijon

France, early 18th century. 1) Balcony railing in Dijon;
2) Balcony railing in the Victoria and Albert Museum, London

France, end of 17th century. Wrought-iron balustrade at Fontainebleau

France, end of 17th century. Wrought-iron balustrade at Fontainebleau

France, end of 17th century. Park gates

England, c. 1700. Grille in the Victoria and Albert Museum, London

198

England, c. 1700. Grille from Hampton Court Palace, now in the Victoria and Albert Museum, London

England, beginning of 18th century. Wrought-iron balustrade, Victoria and Albert Museum, London

England, 18th century. Details from balustrades, Victoria and Albert Museum, London

England, beginning of 18th century. Grilles, Victoria and Albert Museum, London

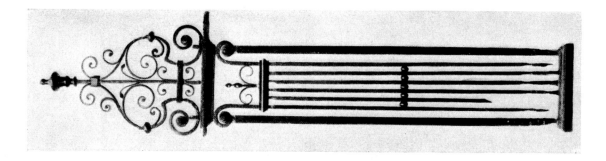

England, beginning of 18th century. Bracket and pilaster, Victoria and Albert Museum, London

England, beginning of 18th century. Brackets and cresting of a grille, Victoria and Albert Museum, London

England, early 18th century. Grille in the Victoria and Albert Museum, London

England, 18th century. Parts of grilles in the Victoria and Albert Museum, London

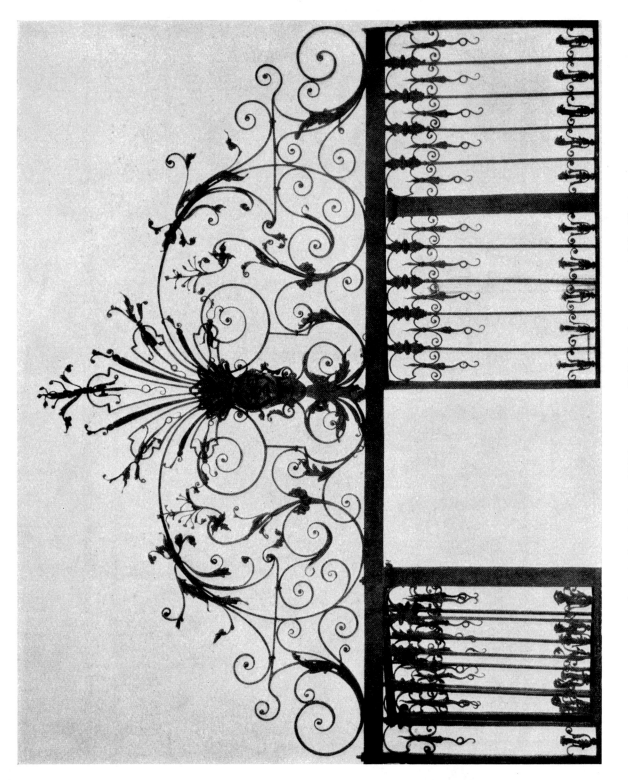

Austria, beginning of 18th century. Grille in the convent of St. Florian

Italy, beginning of 18th century. Grille from Venice in the Schlossmuseum, Berlin

Italy, early 18th century. Fanlight grille and wrought-iron door

Italy, beginning of 18th century. Grilles in the Victoria and Albert Museum, London

Northern Italy, beginning of 18th century. Grille in the Schlossmuseum, Berlin

France, beginning of 18th century. Balcony and part of a grille

212

France, first half of 18th century. Balustrade in an entrance hall in Aix-en-Provence

France, beginning of 18th century. Wrought-iron balustrade in Aix-en-Provence

214

France, 18th century. Detail of a balustrade in Aix-en-Provence

Alsace, 18th century. Signs

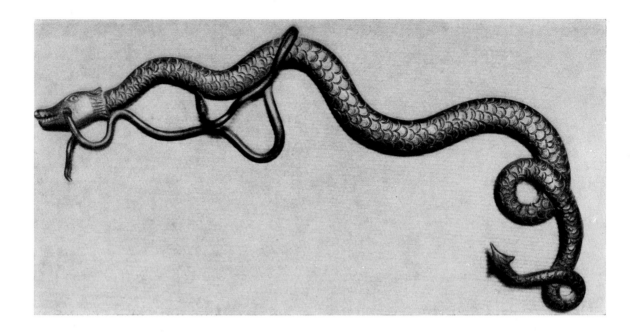

1) and 2) Brackets, France, 18th century. 3) Iron ornament, Germany, 18th century

Germany, beginning of 18th century. Cresting of a counter and part of a grille

Germany, c. 1700. Ornamental grilles from Augsburg

Prague, beginning of 18th century. Grille in the cathedral

Prague, beginning of 18th century. Grille in the Strachow Church

Prague, beginning of 18th century. Grille in the Strachow Church

222

Austria, beginning of 18th century. Grille in the convent church, Stans

Austria, beginning of 18th century. Window grille in Steyr

Austria, beginning of 18th century. Grille in Graz cathedral

Austria, beginning of 18th century. Detail of the grille in Graz cathedral

226

Germany, 18th century. Grille in Heilig-Kreuzkirche, Augsburg

Germany, c. 1712. Grille in St. Ulrichskirche, Augsburg

Germany, c. 1712. Grille in St. Ulrichskirche, Augsburg

Germany, beginning of 18th century. Grille in Constance cathedral

230

Fanlights, early 18th century, from France and South Germany

Brünn (Moravia), beginning of 18th century. Grille in the Franciscan church

Austria, beginning of 18th century, Grille in the collegiate church, Dürnstein

Austria, beginning of 18th century. Grille in the collegiate church, Dürnstein

234

Prague, early 18th century. Grille in the Strachow Church

Austria, c. 1720. Wrought-iron gates Schloss Belvedere, Vienna

Austria, c. 1720. Wrought-iron gates Schloss Belvedere, Vienna

Austria, c. 1720. Wrought-iron gates Schloss Belvedere, Vienna

Germany, first half of 18th century. Fanlight grilles and window-ledge

Germany, c. 1740. Wrought-iron door in the Town Hall, Frankfurt

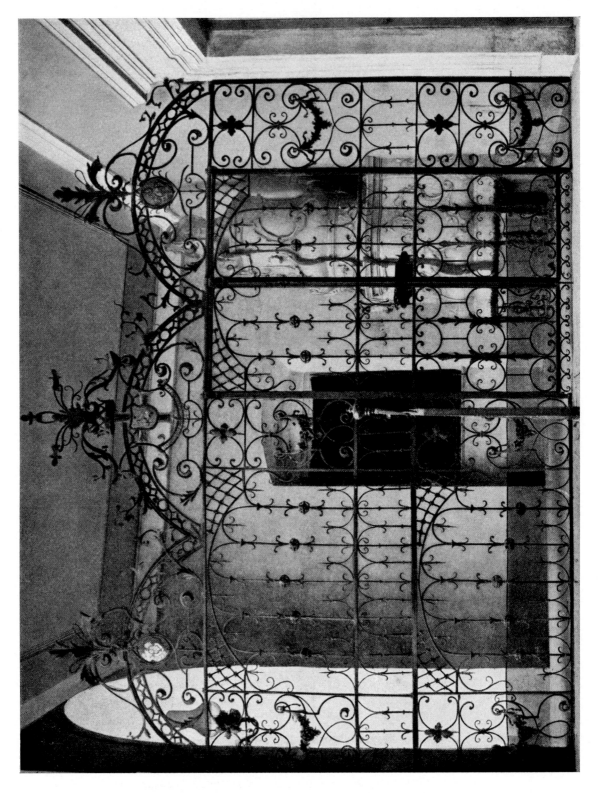

Tyrol, c. 1744. Grille in the House of the Teutonic Order in Bozen

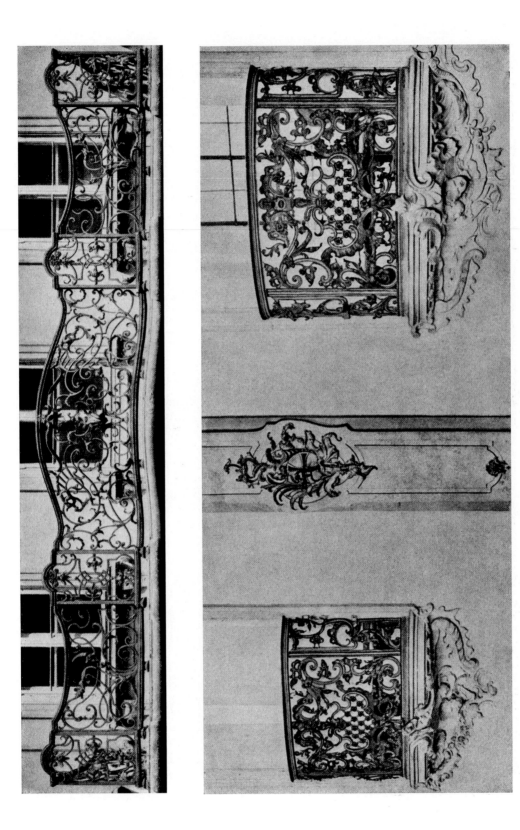

Germany, mid-18th century. 1) Balcony railing from Hannover; 2) from the castle church in Ellingen

Germany, beginning of 18th century. Detail of a grille, Leipzig

Germany, 18th century. Wrought-iron chapel door in Hirschberg (Silesia)

Prague, beginning of 18th century. Iron mounted door, Church of St. Thomas

1) Detail of a grille in Vienna, c. 1744. 2) Fanlight grille from Zurich, c. 1726

246

Prague, beginning of 18th century. Door-handle and knocker on the Palais Clam-Gallas

Door-knocker and door-handles. 1) France, early 18th century; 2) Germany, 17th to 18th century

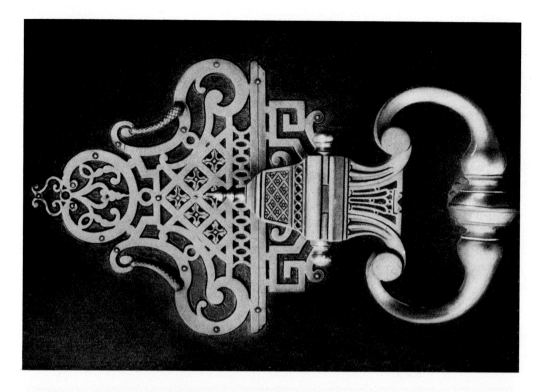

France, 18th century. Door-knockers from Bordeaux

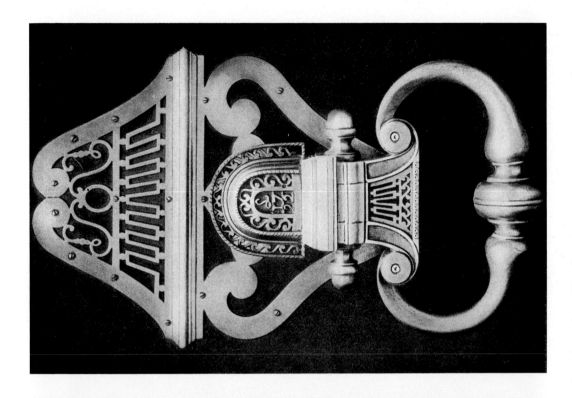

France, 18th century. Door-knockers from Bordeaux

Germany, beginning of 18th century. Door-knocker,
Germanisches Museum, Nuremberg

South Germany, first half of 18th century. Wrought-iron ornaments

Germany, c. 1724. Wrought-iron grille embellishments
Bayerisches Nationalmuseum, Munich

South Germany, mid-18th century. Upper part of a grave-cross,
Bayerisches Nationalmuseum, Munich

Austria, c. 1720. Window grille in Vienna

South Germany, beginning of 18th century. 1) Fanlight grille, 2) Fire-screen

Prague, mid-18th century. Wrought-iron door

South Germany, mid-18th century. Fanlight grilles

Germany, beginning of 18th century. Brackets

Germany, mid-18th century. Brackets

260

Switzerland, first half of 18th century. Grille in Basle

Switzerland, 18th century. Grille in Basle

France, early 18th century. Wrought-iron palace gates in Dampierre (Aube)

France, first half of 18th century. Wrought-iron gates, Château de Bagatelle

France, 18th century. Wrought-iron door in the cathedral, Lyons

France, 18th century. Fanlight grilles in Lyons

France, c. 1730. Grille in Sens, Archbishop's Palace

France, mid-18th century. Grille in the cathedral, Nancy

268

France, mid-18th century. Grille in Nancy, Place Stanislas

France, mid-18th century. Grille in Nancy in the Place Stanislas, by Jean Lamour

France, mid-18th century. Part of the grille in the Place Stanislas in Nancy

France, mid-18th century. Part of the grille in the Place Stanislas in Nancy

272

France, mid-18th century. Chancel grille in the Church of St. John, Lyons

France, mid-18th century. Chancel grille in the Church of St. John, Lyons

France, mid-18th century. Balcony railings from Lyons

Balcony railings, mid-18th century, from Lyons and Zurich (above)

Germany, c. 1743. Baluster work in the Schloss Brühl on the Rhine

Germany, c. 1743. Lantern and grilles in the Schloss Brühl on the Rhine

278

Germany, c. 1750. Grille in Würzburg

Vienna, first half of 18th century. Grille in the Dominican Church

Austria, first half of 18th century. Grille in Salzburg, Franciscan Church

Austria, first half of 18th century. Grille in Salzburg, Franciscan Church

Hungary, mid-18th century. Grille embellishments from Pressburg

Germany, c. 1725. Parts of wrought-iron grilles, Bayerisches Nationalmuseum, Munich

Hungary, mid-18th century. Wrought-iron folding doors

Austria, mid-18th century. Grille in the convent, Reichenberg

Austria, first half of 18th century. Grille in Salzburg, Peterskirche

Germany, mid-18th century. Wrought-iron garden gates in Nuremberg

Germany, c. 1750. Part of a wrought-iron gate in the palace of Würzburg

Germany, c. 1750. Part of a wrought-iron gate in the palace of Würzburg

Germany, c. 1750. Part of a grille from the palace of Würzburg

Germany, c. 1750. Part of a grille from the palace of Würzburg

Germany, c. 1750. Wrought-iron in the palace of Würzburg

Germany, c. 1750. Wrought-iron in the palace of Würzburg

Hungary, mid-18th century. Wrought-iron gate from Heves

Germany, mid-18th century. Wrought-iron gate on the church, Roggenburg

Germany, mid-18th century. Wrought-iron gate, Schloss Wellenberg

Germany, mid-18th century. Wrought-iron gate in Oberzell

Switzerland, mid-18th century. Wrought-iron gates in Zurich

Switzerland, 18th century. Grille in the Rittergasse in Basle

Switzerland, mid-18th century. Window grilles in Basle

Window grilles from Rothenburg and Basle, second half of 18th century

Switzerland, c. 1770. Chancel grille in the collegiate church of St. Gallen

South Germany, c. 1760. Grille in the church, Ober-Marchthal

304

Germany, 1720-1750. Bracket, cresting for a grille and grave-cross

Fanlight grilles from South Germany and Switzerland. First half of 18th century

Italy, beginning of 18th century. Detail of a church railing in Bologna

France, second half of 18th century.
Detail of a church railing in St. Germain l'Auxerrois, Paris

France, second half of 18th century. Wrought-iron balustrade, Grand Trianon, Versailles

France, second half of 18th century. Wrought-iron balustrade, Château de Compiègne

France, second half of 18th century. Wrought-iron stair railing, in the Admiralty, Paris

1) Austria. Fanlight grille in Znaim;
2) France. Wrought-iron balustrade in Dijon; second half of 18th century

France, second half of 18th century. Grille in École militaire, Paris

France, second half of 18th century. Wrought-iron gates in Palais de Justice, Paris

314

Germany, second half of 18th century. Grille, Schloss Veitshöchheim

Germany, second half of 18th century. Schloss Veitshöchheim, cresting of a grille

316

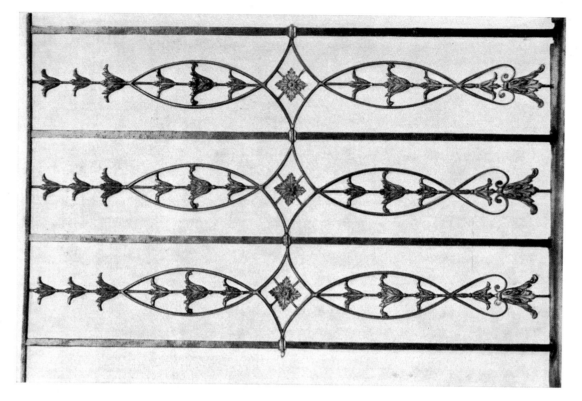

1) Window grille from Austria; 2) Detail of a grille from England. Second half of 18th century

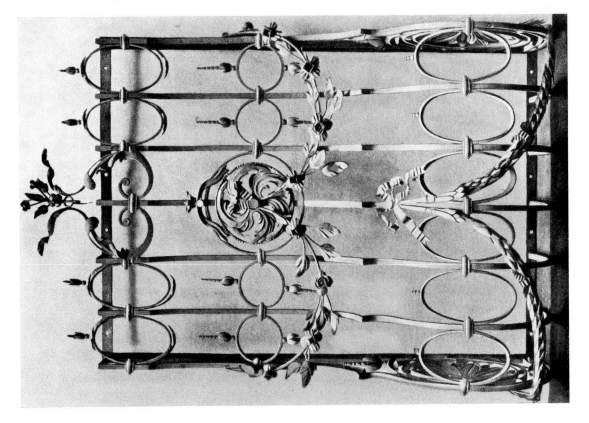

South Germany and Switzerland. Window grilles, second half of 18th century

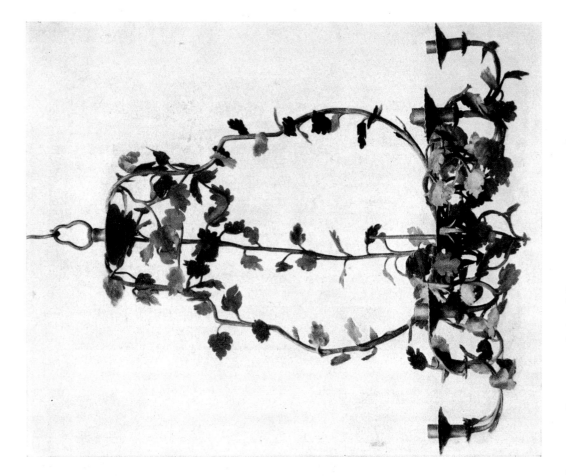

Germany, 18th century. Lantern and chandelier

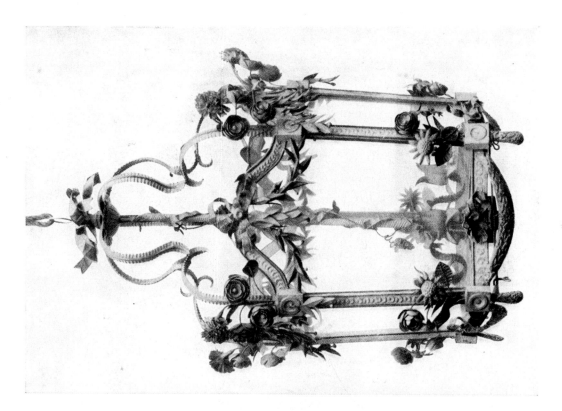

Germany, second half of 18th century. Wrought-iron lanterns

Germany, second half of 18th century. 1) and 3) Fanlight grilles, 2) cresting of a counter